HELPING NETWORKS AND HUMAN SERVICES

Volume 128, Sage Library of Social Research

RECENT VOLUMES IN
SAGE LIBRARY OF SOCIAL RESEARCH

HELPING NETWORKS and HUMAN SERVICES

Charles Froland
Diane L. Pancoast
Nancy J. Chapman
Priscilla J. Kimboko

Foreword by Alice H. Collins

Volume 128
SAGE LIBRARY OF
SOCIAL RESEARCH

 **SAGE PUBLICATIONS**   Beverly Hills   London

For information address:

SAGE Publications, Inc.
275 South Beverly Drive
Beverly Hills, California 90212

SAGE Publications Ltd
28 Banner Street
London EC1Y 8QE, England

Printed in the United States of America

Library of Congress Cataloging in Publication Data

Main entry under title:

Helping networks and human services.

   (Sage library of social research; v. 128)
   Bibliography: p.
   1. Social service—Case studies. 2. Social structure —Case studies. 3. Helping behavior—Case studies. 4. Volunteer workers in social service—Case studies. I. Froland, Charles. II. Series.

HV40.H49	361.3	81-9152
ISBN 0-8039-1625-6		AACR2
ISBN 0-8039-1626-4 (pbk.)		

FIRST PRINTING

CONTENTS

This book is dedicated to Arthur C. Emlen,
Director of the Regional Research Institute for
Human Services at Portland State University,
whose inspiration and wit sustained us all.

HELPING NETWORKS AND HUMAN SERVICES

Volume 128, Sage Library of Social Research

ACKNOWLEDGMENTS

The research reported here was supported by a grant from the Office of Human Development Services, Department of Health and Human Services, under Grant 18-P-00088. James Dolson, our Project Officer for the grant, deserves thanks for his kind help in providing support for the research. We would also like to thank our consultants, Alice H. Collins, Benjamin Gottlieb, and Sarah Smith for their comments during the course of our research. Paul Parker and Michael Bayley of Sheffield University provided us with invaluable assistance that enriched our work with the lessons and experiences of efforts currently underway in England. The greatest amount of gratitude, however, must go to the many staff members in each of the agencies we studied who so generously gave of their time, providing the insights and first-hand knowledge which have come to form the basis of this book. The conclusions we have drawn remain, of course, the responsibility of the authors.

Without the institutional support of the Regional Research Institute for Human Services at Portland State University, our study could never have become a book. Victoria Mercer, our secretary, deserves a special thanks for suffering through the research with good humor. Nicole Burkholder and Katie Liedtke were most gracious in typing the manuscript under the special burdens imposed by multiple authorship.

FOREWORD

Helping Networks and Human Services articulates and integrates a broad set of practices and policies concerning the relationship between formal services and informal caregiving. It moves the development of this important area of social policy from the stage of exploratory, demonstration and research efforts to that of consciously formulated, widely applicable strategies based on a common philosophy.

As a participant in the development of the social work profession for half a century, I have long felt that the profession was moving too far away from its beginnings in settlement houses and voluntary societies. In the process, welfare services were becoming increasingly less sensitive to the real needs and capacities of the people they were intended to serve. My first opportunity to see what could be done to reverse this process was a demonstration project intended to strengthen family day care.

When, in 1965, Eunice Watson and I began to apply our theories about the potential value of professional consultation with informal helping networks in family day care (Collins and Watson, 1969), we felt the excitement and frustration of all pioneers. It was gratifying to confirm that helping networks we had envisaged among day care givers and users actually existed and that they often revolved around key helpers who were amenable and even enthusiastic about accepting us, professional social workers, as their partners.

As we got better acquainted with these helpers we recognized their matchmaking and advice-giving functions as being a part of their way of life and enormously effective. We found it no challenge to maintain the position we had taken at the outset—that we would refrain from interfering with professional training or advice and would encourage informal helpers to continue to function in their own style which would rarely resemble that of professionals.

We found it exciting to be evolving an approach that dealt with problems of prevention that had long seemed insoluble, while at the same time we were baffled by issues that the work raised. When we looked to the literature to learn from the experience of others, we found that only a few such projects had been reported. It was amazing to note how closely some of them paralleled ours, and they offered reassurance that the idea of working with informal helping networks seemed worth testing to many professionals in widely separated communities. But we still could not answer the many questions that inevitably followed when we described our work to others in the hopes that they might want to attempt similar innovations. Was our success based on the neighborhood we had chosen? On aspects of our style of working with informal helpers that were unconscious and therefore not replicable elsewhere? How did our approach differ from the well-known practice of community organization? Or from the use of paraprofessionals in agencies (an approach no less enthusiastically advocated although failing to live up to its promise)? How could informal helpers be found and what could professionals offer them since they were already doing an excellent job on their own? How could we justify the unquestionable breach of confidentiality at a number of levels that work with informal helping networks involved?

It became depressingly clear to us that what we saw as a new and promising way of reaching the many in need of help, unreached at the time, was not to be incorporated into practice solely from our account of it. We feared our lessons would take their place beside many other demonstration programs, successful in their small way but not generalizable and now locked away in hundreds of file drawers. We were only too well aware that what was needed was a careful study of a number of similar efforts with conclusions based not only on the subjective lessons of their practitioners but on sophisticated, objective research that could compare, contrast, categorize, and evaluate the wide range of informal helping networks that might be available.

Just such a study is reported in highly readable form in *Helping Networks and Human Services*. The authors have studied the innovations of thirty agencies working with informal helping networks. The lessons of agency staff have been analyzed from many points of view, including reviews of studies elsewhere that bear on the subject. Case examples drawn from the reports of the agencies studied enliven the text and illuminate the research findings.

The authors have not been content to state their findings alone but have gone on to draw some important conclusions. The book sets the innovations of the thirty agencies into the context of a far-reaching debate about the respective role of the public and private sectors in the provision of human services—a debate that has often centered around the costliness of public services in general. Unquestionably, work with informal helping networks is economically advantageous in its ability to extend the reach of expensive professional services. And while this may prove a cogent reason for the adoption of the concept, it must fall to professionals to interpret the method as having much greater potential than simply saving tax dollars. It may well require the reexamination of the basic assumptions which underlie the elaborate structure of social welfare services that has been constructed in the past fifty years.

Only a few books have contributed to major changes in the philosophy and direction of public services in the past. I believe this book will take its place among those seminal works.

—Alice H. Collins
Author, Consultant,
and Former Director
of Day-Care
Neighbor Service,
Portland

Chapter 1

INTRODUCTION

Since the turn of the century, the public sector in the United States has taken on a growing list of responsibilities for addressing the social and health needs of citizens. While in earlier times problems were handled in the public sector only by exception, the last half-century has witnessed an expansion in the role of the state as a guarantor of public well-being. The state is now expected to play the leading role in the planning and provision of human services.

The assumption of greater public responsibility for human needs may have proceeded to the point where we have lost sight of the substantial role that informal caregiving and mutual aid still play in the daily lives of clients and those who manage not to become clients. We may forget that family members, friends, neighbors, clergy, storekeepers, bartenders and others who might be labelled "just plain citizens" often comprise an informal circle of helpers for a person experiencing problems and that formal help from agencies and trained professionals is sought only as a last resort (Gourash, 1978; Kulka, Veroff & Douvan, 1979).

Amid predictions of a breakdown of traditional social bonds and popular characterizations of the "me" generation of the 1970s, evidence that personal relationships in everyday life remain the primary source of caring for people can be looked on with optimism. Growing recognition of this fact has called into question the prevailing view of the residual role of the private, voluntary sector in social policy, and has given rise to increasing debate about the appropriate boundaries of human service organizations (see National Commission on Neighborhoods, 1979; President's Commission on Mental Health, 1978; Wingspread Report, 1978). Although expressed in a variety of terms, the debate centers around the question of responsibility for care. One side emphasizes the need for family and community responsibility, while the opposition calls for state intervention and public responsibility. It seems clear, however, that no one source of care—public, private, or voluntary—can by itself adequately meet the needs of dependent populations; that scarce resources will not support an indefinite expansion of public commitments; and that neither large scale public retrenchment nor public takeover constitutes a feasible course of action. Finding ways to share the responsibility for care between the public and private sectors and between family and state has become a more desirable goal to many (Moroney, 1980; Parker, 1980).

Sharing Responsibility for Care

This book begins with the assumption that shared responsibility for care is possible and sets about the task of exploring what that can mean in program design and policy. We will explore the idea that professionals can and should develop mutually beneficial ways to combine their skills with the strengths of informal helpers in providing a system of community care for people in need.

Our discussion draws primarily from the findings of a two-year study we conducted to identify and assess program strategies which human service agencies might adopt to collaborate with informal helping networks. We looked at thirty agencies that had developed innovative programs to address the needs of such populations as the elderly, the physically and developmentally disabled, children, youth and families, and the mentally ill, as well as serving the wider community. In selecting programs for study, our concern was not to be comprehensive or even representative, but to provide insights into the range of problems encountered and the strategies being employed in order to develop a framework for further definition and refinement of practice in this area. The agencies comprised a diverse and rich mix of program examples from urban and rural settings across the United States. Some operated under public auspices and others as private nonprofit agencies. They varied widely in such factors as funding sources, size, and length of operation (see Appendix A for a complete discussion of the sample characteristics and methodology of the study).

We visited these agencies, talked to staff members and informal helpers, and studied reports. We wrote up case studies on each agency, trying to be as faithful to the spirit of the program as we could and using their own words whenever possible. We have incorporated excerpts from these case studies throughout the book, setting them off to make them obvious and numbering them so that it would be possible for a reader to trace which excerpts came from a particular case. Appendix B provides a listing and brief description of the cases.

In addition to lessons derived from agency experience, we also draw on relevant literature in order to provide a framework of important concepts which underlie our specific findings. We have adopted a broad perspective on the issues raised by the experiences of these thirty agencies in order to fully reflect the possibilities of this emerging field of practice. In this chapter we will set out the foundations of this perspective by discussing the importance of helping networks, outlining the differences between formal and informal helping and presenting the basic elements for a new collaboration between human services and helping networks.

The Importance of Helping Networks
for Individuals and Communities

We have chosen to use the shorthand term "helping networks" to describe a wide range of informal helping activities that staff in the agencies we studied have sought to identify, support, and reinforce. Our use of the term is more than a convenience, however, since we believe that emphasizing informal helping within the context of a *network* of relationships has distinct conceptual advantages to more traditional ways of viewing social relationships. The concept of a network in its most general form draws our attention to the *structure* of relationships among a set of actors as well as the specific *exchanges* which take place among them and the *roles* they play with each other. Networks describe social relationships in fairly concrete terms. Fischer (1977:33) has described networks as "a specified set of links among social actors."

A network can only be described after criteria have been determined for defining what types of relationships are of interest. These may be the relationships that one individual has with others in a personal network, or the ties that link a number of "nodes," where the nodes may be some combination of individuals, families, groups, organizations, or other social units. This way of viewing social relationships focuses on the actual interactions of daily living, the specific relationships that constitute a primary group or support system. It does not imply awareness on anyone's part of a role or status vis-à-vis another person, nor does it imply that the actions of various persons are organized, interdependent, or directed to a common goal. They may be any of these things but they need not be in order to be described in network terms. For a practitioner in an agency contemplating an intervention at the client or community level, analyzing the situation in network terms offers the dual advantages of specificity in terms of actors and actions and an absence of confining categories which can lead to a priori decisions as to who should or should not be important.

Friendship, the exchange of advice and support, patronage, and referral are examples of the types of relationships which can define a particular network. Our study defined the relevant focus of a *helping* network as that set of social relationships which provide care, support, and other forms of assistance for people who experience social and health-related problems of the sort which might also be of concern to human service agencies. Even the most socially isolated individuals and the most anomic communities seem to have a few relationships of this sort. We all use our networks when we need information or special assistance. In turn, our networks influence us by channeling and shaping the kinds of information we take in. They also require certain forms of reciprocation as well as the ongoing effort of maintaining the linkages. Networks are a part of our sense of who we are.

In addition to shedding light on the actual resources available to an individual or community, a network perspective reveals the patterned regularity that underlies the apparent randomness of daily interaction. Interconnecting relationships among individuals are important for understanding the whole network, and have consequences for the members even when these patterns are not apparent to those within the network. As Paul Craven and Barry Wellman (1973:69) note, "Upon meeting for the first time, members who have been up to that point only indirectly linked in the network may find that they have many friends or acquaintances in common and have been, unawares, sharing information, norms and values for a long time." Many of the "small world" experiences we all have are not so much examples of chance and coincidence as they are illustrations of the pathways within networks. This structural stability is, of course, an important source of predictability for individuals, but it also provides a firm foundation on which programs which interweave formal and informal helping can be built.

Evidence culled from a wide range of fields of study suggests the general importance of informal helping networks to individual health and well-being in a variety of situations relevant to human services professionals. The influence of a network on the individual is multifaceted and has the potential for negative as well as positive effects. Informal caregivers in an individual's personal network, made up of family, friends, and neighbors, remain the primary reference point for those seeking and obtaining help (Gourash, 1978). Studies conducted over the last several decades show this source of help to be relatively unchanged in its dimensions (Kulka, Veroff & Douvan, 1979). An individual's social network is a major factor in defining the nature of problems, providing help, influencing what sources of outside help will be obtained, and aiding in adjustment to a wide range of acute and chronic problems (Froland, 1979). Moreover, individual reports suggest that the help received from family, relatives, and neighbors is about as helpful as that received from professionals (Lieberman & Mullan, 1978) and, in some instances, more helpful (Eddy, Paap & Glad, 1970). Informal helping networks are well suited for providing concrete advice, emotional reassurance, an immediate response, long term caring, and everyday assistance (Litwak, 1978a).

Evidence that informal helping continues to be important to people is also found when one looks at the informal helping networks found among neighborhood groups and mutual aid or self-help groups. Grassroots groups have increased dramatically over the last several decades; a recent poll shows that more than 50 percent of urban dwellers had participated in local group efforts (Gallup, 1978). Self-help and mutual aid groups have proliferated to the extent that they may well number in excess of several hundred thousand (Katz & Bender, 1976).

The functions performed by informal associations are diverse, meeting both individual and collective needs for social integration. Mutual aid groups provide a forum for sharing common problems, experiences, and interests wherein the credibility of "having been there before" serves to provide support, reassurance, and identity for members (Durman, 1976). Collectivities formed because of shared backgrounds or present circumstances offer a vehicle for "reciprocal helping" (Abrams, 1978; Bayley, 1978) in which the distinction between those being helped and those helping is ignored and an emphasis is placed on mutuality and shared effort. Participants are not viewed as "cases" with "presenting problems," but rather as experts on their own situations with much to offer one another in a common task. Further, the functions of local primary groups, or "social blocs" as they have recently been called, are prized as a mediating factor in relating individual experience and influence to larger social institutions (Berger & Neuhaus, 1977; Janowitz & Suttles, 1978). Whether this takes the form of advocacy in relation to a local issue (such as "redlining" or zoning policies), lobbying for the needs and rights of a specific subpopulation (e.g., educational policies for handicapped children, transportation for the elderly), or simply being represented in decisions about local policies and programs, rights and responsibilities. The position taken here is that

> by themselves, bureaucratic norms, universalistic standards and the ideals of democracy seem uncompelling unless they are endorsed . . . in the smaller confines in which individuals can feel the consequences of their action . . . (and) experienced as consequential for others who are sufficiently close to arouse "empathy." . . . It is in the local community that individuals have the opportunity . . . both to internalize and aggregate the diverse gains and costs of public policy [Janowitz & Suttles, 1978:88].

This broad-ranging review reveals both the diversity and flexibility of the concept of informal helping networks. The concept encompasses a wide variety of different types of relationships and kinds of exchanges from psychological to political. It suggests that a richer and more realistic view of the resources available to people is possible and can be brought to bear more systematically in reaching human service objectives when networks are taken into account.

Relating Professional Services and Informal Helping Networks

Professionals are currently developing or modifying models of practice which by various means recognize and incorporate the implicit roles that networks may perform with respect to individual clients, organizations, communities or neighborhoods. These changes have most often been motivated by a philosophical belief in the importance of personal relationships for client well being and developed through a process of discovery and innovation in the course of providing services. Since relatively few have been guided by available research evidence regarding the functioning of helping networks, the emerging models of practice tend to be hybrids of conventional service delivery strategies which have been modified to incorporate network ideas (see reviews in Erickson, 1975; Parker, 1977; Schon, 1977; Trimble, 1980).

While we often think of the efforts of human service agencies to work with informal helping networks as a recent innovation, there are in fact a number of historical antecedents with similar aims. For example, at the turn of the century, settlement house workers discussed the feasibility of enlisting neighborhood representatives who were performing key helping roles informally (Coit, 1892); now we speak of enlisting "indigenous leaders" or "natural helpers" (Collins and Pancoast, 1976). In 1915, a "social unit plan" was proposed which would establish working relationships between representatives of groups having special skills or service knowledge with representatives of small, primary groups of local residents (Lubove, 1965); now we see proposals for "community empowerment" or "mediating structures" which embody the same principles and intentions for working with local communities (Berger & Neuhaus; 1977; Biegel & Spence, 1978). Reviews of the history of community grassroots efforts (Cox & Garvin, 1972; Perlman, 1976; Smith & Freedman, 1972), self-help and mutual aid groups (Katz & Bender, 1976) and work with paraprofessionals or nonprofessionals (Gershon & Biller, 1977; Levine, Tulkin, Intagliata, Perry & Whitsun, 1978) show that there has been a persistent fascination with the idea of relating formally organized services to informal sources of help.

Perhaps the main stumbling block faced in trying to find ways to link professionals and informal helpers is that they have potentially radically different understandings of what care means. In finding linkages, we are asked to cross invisible boundaries between the organized and the communal, "the public world of the bureaucrat and the private world of mothers" (Abrams, 1978).

The formal world of organized, professional services is largely comprised of services that are publicly mandated or sponsored whether they are state-administered or provided through chartered intermediaries such as private nonprofit organizations. As such, formal care also includes private practice, when controlled either by regulation or reimbursement, as well as services provided by voluntary organizations which receive governmental financial support either directly or indirectly through tax transfers. Formal services operate under a system of explicit categories for assessing need or eligibility, formal rules of procedure, specialization and formal coordination among helping roles, definitions and expectations associated with client or consumer status, consistency of standards for treating problems independent of personal characteristics of the client, and objectively stated criteria for what constitutes success or progress.

These formal prescriptions governing who is helped and how help is given stand in contrast to the rules that implicitly govern the informal care provided by kin, friends and neighbors, indigenous or natural helpers, and informal self-help or mutual aid activities. Informal helping is voluntary and is relatively unorganized and spontaneous (Wolfenden Report, 1978). It is not a one-way activity but a mutual flow which involves the receipt of help as well as giving. Help is provided as part of a continuing set of mutual exchanges that comprise a larger system of rights and obligations within a primary group, neighborhood, or culture (see Lenrow, 1976; Riessman, 1976). Expressed in terms of classical sociology, the distinction draws from the contrasts posed by Weber between bureaucratic versus primary group relations (see Litwak, 1978b) and from Parsons's pattern variables characterizing action based on universalistic versus particularistic criteria (see Abrams, 1978).

An attempt to link formal and informal modes of support is likely to result in a clashing of two different cultures: one seeking the reliability of formal rules and routine procedures, the other emphasizing the privacy of unspoken rules and spontaneous activity (Abrams, 1978). Norms of exchange, conceptions of problems and solutions, and beliefs about authority and responsibility are considerably different and potentially at odds. These theoretical representations of the contrast between formal and informal support suggest that attempts to combine the efforts of each type of support will always encounter basic conflicts (Froland, 1980).

By and large the two worlds of care *are* separate and independent most of the time. People generally meet most of their daily needs through informal relationships and expect to "play by the rules" when they choose (or are forced) to rely on formal sources of help. However, there are also many instances in which these distinctions are blurred or where the need arises to achieve a blend of the characteristics of the two types of care: when a local group of priests requests family life education sessions from a family service agency for parishioners; when an agency providing home-based services for the elderly receives a request for a homemaker but does not want to disturb the web of informal caring already in place; when a self-help group decides to seek funding from the United Way in order to hire a staff person and publicize its activities; when a settlement house decides it has lost touch with a neighborhood and wants to reestablish a presence.

Clearly, it is not impossible for formal and informal sources of support to complement each other; indeed, as Litwak (1978a) has argued, exchange between both types is necessary in dealing with the various tasks of care. Such an exchange, however, depends for success on a better understanding of what each side has to offer the other.

Evidence reviewed earlier shows that informal helping networks have been considered fundamental as a first line of defense and as a building block for social integration. However, informal helping also has a number of limitations. When compared with the standards of care that prevail within formally organized services, informal helping networks simply do not provide enough care for enough people. Not everyone has a caring social network, ties with a neighborhood, or an inclination to participate within a network of mutual aid. In addition, the particularism of informal helping networks can be exclusive as well as inclusive. Continuity and reliability of care within the informal system of family, caring neighbors, and devoted friends can also be problematic, as limited knowledge about problems and lack of resources undermine the ability to be of assistance. An ongoing need for aid may lead to feelings of being burdensome and subsequent rejection or withdrawal of support. Collective efforts often have a short life, withering when membership changes or interest wanes. Further, the informal quest for empowerment can lead to disenfranchising other groups with different interests in the competition for power and resources. Finally, the emphasis on self-reliance and independence can often obscure broader concerns for social welfare (Janowitz & Suttles, 1979).

One line of argument holds that the present constitution of governmental and professional services is a direct response to the failures of the informal sector (Wolfenden Report, 1978). The formal sector emphasizes equity in the coverage and provision of care. Programs are established to promote the transfer and diffusion of risks to relieve the burden of chronic and catastrophic situations. Organization permits the development and efficient use of specialized resources, while systems of accountability and electoral representation provide for responsiveness and accessibility to power.

Formally organized services also have limitations, however. First, formal services are costly either to society, if publicly funded, or to recipients, if offered on a fee for services basis. In contrast, the informal system typically is based on the mutual exchange typical of a barter economy. Because the formal system is large, publicly funded, and often regulated at the federal level, it is often neither required nor able to be responsive to the idiosyncratic needs of particular individuals or communities. The result is a system of care that many potential clients perceive as unresponsive to their needs and demeaning to accept, since they are defined solely as a recipient of aid rather than as part of a mutual exchange system (Wolfenden Report, 1978).

The respective strengths and weaknesses of each sector of caring are often viewed as being complementary (Litwak, 1978a). Professionals are best able to handle problems requiring technical knowledge, expertise, and objectivity, while the informal sector can respond to problems requiring long term adjustment and emotional support. The informal sector should participate in local affairs, but the public sector will need to provide vehicles for equalizing representation and balancing competing interests and claims for services. While this compatibility between formal and informal roles does occur, the relationship is not always quite so simple and harmonious a partnership. Complementary functions often give way to contradictory perspectives about who should handle what problems and in what way.

Alternatives to Collaboration

Since the implicit and explicit rules that govern formal and informal caregiving are at times conflicting as well as complementary, attempts to develop a relationship between the two are often difficult. The resulting interaction often does not fit the ideal model of collaboration, as illustrated by four alternative modes of inter-action: conflict, competition, cooptation, and coexistence.

The conflict mode occurs when public and private assessments of responsibilities and the appropriateness of care are at odds. Examples of conflict over the degree of public responsibility for care are numerous, as illustrated by the civil rights and social action move-ments of the 1960s that attempted to foster greater public responsi-bility for ending segregation and discrimination, and for public assistance. Questions involving the responsibility of relatives for individuals receiving public assistance have never been completely resolved (Bell, 1967). In other cases, the conflict involves the appro-priate form of public care. Parent-rights efforts concerning educa-tional policies for the handicapped and developmentally disabled, and moves toward large-scale deinstitutionalization of the mentally and physically disabled have been based in part on a conflict over the balance between formal and informal care. Conflict can also stem from public reaction to informal practices as seen in the posture taken toward such self-help groups as Synanon, the Network Against Psychiatric Assault, and other groups considered questionable in light of current standards of care. The policing and regulatory functions performed by the formal sector have brought it into conflict with practices of many informal caregivers such as midwives (Rubin, 1975).

A competitive mode of interaction is often adopted in situations where there is a common perception of need but different assessments of the responsibility or the capacity of available alternatives to provide care. The clearest example here is in the field of day care, where there is a tacit acceptance of competition between formal, governmentally sponsored day care centers and the informal pro-vision of family day care (Emlen, 1970). Very often, competition between the formal and informal sectors is considered a healthy way to promote innovation or to provide alternative options for care.

Cooptation as a mode of interaction is not usually intentional, but rather emerges over time out of collaborative efforts. Community groups initially trying to change local services often wind up providing service themselves or, when successful in obtaining funding or formal recognition, become compromised in their ability to be advocates for institutional change (Dearlove, 1974; Santiago, 1972). The dilemma faced by citizen representatives and consumer boards suggests a similar trend toward cooptation (Parker, 1972). Experience with the use of "indigenous paraprofessionals" as bridges to poor communities has shown that informal helpers tend to take on professional roles and come to identify more with the interests of formally organized service agencies than with the community (Levine et al., 1978). What started out as an attempt to foster participation and responsiveness moved in the direction of greater alignment with the values and perspectives of institutional and professional services.

The mode of coexistence represents a choice not to interact, whether stemming from ignorance, benign disregard, or a judgment that there are no benefits to be gained from interaction. This is perhaps the most popular or characteristic relationship between the formal and informal sectors of care. It is illustrated by the fact that, while there is widespread recognition of the helping patterns that occur within families, neighborhoods, and mutual aid groups, there are relatively few efforts being made by formal services to make a connection with these informal activities. In some instances, the care that occurs is simply too informal and spontaneous to be taken into account by formal efforts. When formal care has been rejected, as in the case of mutual aid and self-help groups that have been formed in an antagonistic reaction to professional services, there is little motivation on either side to join forces (Katz & Bender, 1976). Finally, coexistence may simply be an acknowledgement that the aims of informal caring efforts are outside of the bounds of public policy (Durman, 1976). Mutual aid groups concerned with consciousness raising, personal growth, or self-improvement illustrate aspects of help found in the informal sector for which there is neither an acceptance of nor a great demand for public responsibility.

Toward a Partnership

Throughout this book, we emphasize the development of methods for professionals working in formal human service agencies to interact with informal helping networks in ways that are mutually supportive and synergistic rather than competitive or destructive. Variously described as a collegial partnership (Froland, Pancoast, Chapman & Kimboko, 1979), or more ambitiously as a process of interweaving (Bayley, 1973), collaboration between formal and informal systems of care seems to be a particularly difficult venture to sustain and, over time, often tends to move in the direction of other modes of interaction. Bayley (1978: 2) has provided a concise description of the aims of collaboration:

> The caring done by families, friends, neighbors or larger, more organized groups of people is seen, recognized and acknowledged. An attempt is made to see both particular needs and the strengths and limitations of the informal resources available. The social services seek to interweave their help so as to use and strengthen the help already given, make good the limitations and meet the needs. It is not a question of . . . plugging the gaps but rather of . . . working with society to enable society to close the gaps.

The best examples of collaboration often arise on an ad hoc basis, as when a professional is able to form a consultative relationship with a neighborhood helper who provides friendly reassurance to elderly neighbors (Smith, 1975); an outreach team is able to develop an informal support system of hotel managers, board and care operators, bartenders and grocery clerks in promoting the community adjustment of the chronically mentally ill (Pancoast, Froland & Collins, 1980); or when informal working relationships are established between mutual aid or self-help groups and professionals (Cutler, 1979).

Collaboration offers the best possibility for an ongoing and productive relationship between formal and informal systems of care although competition and coexistence may at times also be legitimate responses to some problems. Any relationship must be built on an understanding of the strengths and weaknesses of each system. Our description of what we propose as a partnership is based on a synthesis of the experiences of staff in the thirty agencies we have studied, as well as a wider range of work going on in the field. Our interest has been to pose possibilities, raise issues, and offer conceptual clarity to policy makers and practitioners. We do not consider the results from our study as statements of conclusive proof but rather as providing a basis for refining the exploratory efforts of those already working in the field and to suggest program options for those who recognize the need to expand the public's role in the provision of human services.

Each of the chapters in this book explores different considerations regarding what is involved in developing a beneficial relationship between formal and informal sources of care. We present the findings of our study by first looking at types of informal helpers and what each can do, and at some of the motivations underlying their activities. We then present the major features of the partnership we envision by describing the variety of ways informal sources of help were involved in agency services, the program strategies developed to promote this involvement, and the relationships formed between agency staff and informal helpers in the community. Case examples are frequently provided to illustrate how programs may work in practice.

Having described the basic elements of the relationships we observed in our sample of thirty agencies, we examine the costs and consequences of different program strategies and how these varied according to the problem or task being addressed. We then discuss how program strategies can be integrated in practice and describe the benefits of doing so. Next, we put the idea of a partnership in context by discussing how relationships between professionals and informal helpers are influenced by aspects of a particular agency and by characteristics of a neighborhood with which an agency may be working. Further, we look at the way other agencies influence an agency's work with informal helpers.

The last two chapters of the book discuss the findings of the study in a broader context of program policy and practice. Here, we look at implications for the role of professionals and possible modifications in traditional practice roles. Finally, we discuss policy considerations for agency decision makers in designing or implementing ways to involve informal helpers in a system of community care.

Chapter 2

INFORMAL HELPING NETWORKS

The biblical story of the Good Samaritan is probably the best known model of helpfulness: a person sees someone else in need and provides help voluntarily with no apparent anticipation of personal reward or gain. The general assumption is that such altruism is exhibited only by exceptional persons who are disposed to come to the aid of others because of unique personality factors. There are a variety of other situations, however, in which people interact on an informal basis that have positive consequences for others; the motivations for this helping are varied. Some helping occurs on a spontaneous basis between people who are strangers; other types of informal helping occur within long standing relationships between family members or among friends. Help is also provided by those who become familiar strangers—people seen regularly in the course of daily activities but with whom a formal relationship has not developed, e.g., bus drivers, store clerks, waitresses. Except for those extraordinary good deeds that occasionally come to the public's eye as human interest stories in the press, most informal helping is given and received with little or no comment.

Whatever the strengths of informal helping, there are also problems that affect people for which professional expertise, officially sanctioned procedures and formally established service organizations may be required. Physical handicaps, severe illness, psychological and emotional difficulties, and economic hardships are some of the needs that can tax the abilities of family, friends, and others who usually provide assistance and create a demand for the formal provision of services. However the necessity for formal services should not blind us to the importance of informal helping.

From the perspective of program and policy in human services, the important question is: What can be expected of informal sources of help for problems which may also require formal services? The strengths and limitations of informal helping can be understood by getting a better view of the kinds of activities that make up informal helping and the variety of influences that shape the way help is provided. It is important to keep in mind that the informal helping discussed in this chapter is seen through the eyes of agency staff and, as such, is not necessarily representative of the total range of informal caring that exists (see Curry & Young, 1978). This perspective, however, is very likely to represent the types of informal caregiving that are most relevant and accessible to formal, professional caregivers.

Informal Helpers: What do they do?

Several researchers have looked at the question of how people help each other on an informal basis and the nature of the support and assistance that is provided (Cantor, 1975; Gottlieb, 1978; Hirsch, 1980). Drawing from this work and from an analysis of the specific examples of helping activities found among the agencies in our study, we identified four types of helping. The first type is caretaking, which includes providing material assistance (from money or tools to the proverbial cup of sugar) and services such as help with housework or transportation. Caretaking can also involve a very informal process of "keeping an eye out for" an elderly person, local children, or the house of an absent neighbor. The second category is friendship, and ranges from simply chatting to providing emotional support for someone with a problem. The third category, problem-solving, includes giving advice directly and linking an individual to others who can help solve the problem. Finally, some helpers are involved in joint action. This may be cooperative communal activity, such as building a community meeting house or fundraising, or an active process of advocacy, organizing, or planning that will have long-range benefit for others.

In each of the agencies we studied, there were examples which illustrated the breadth of activities, tasks, and other forms of assistance which informal helpers could provide. The following examples come from a program working within an urban community in which much of the helping is done in a neighborhood setting:

Mrs. B. is a middle-aged, married black woman whose own children are grown. She and her husband have a good, very traditional marriage, and she respects his wishes and his schedule in her helping efforts. Yet, out of a sense of Christian duty (and a kind heart), she reaches out to her neighbors in a variety of ways. She keeps an eye out for the blind couple who live next door, helps them with a variety of home maintenance activities, and checks out strangers knocking at their door. Another neighbor she helps is a young, single mother who often needs advice and emotional support concerning her children and other personal problems. Every person on her block regards Mrs. B. as someone whom others can turn to for help. She sees herself as doing very little and is somewhat amazed at the attention being given to her.

Mrs. P. is another helper who is more indirect in the services she renders. She is a person who collects information about programs of every type that might benefit people in her circle of friends and neighbors. She keeps files on these programs, and often calls agencies for more detailed information. Mrs. P. is also active in efforts to organize a summer work project for young people in the neighborhood.

Ms. S. is a young, single black mother who keeps an eye out for the kids on her block, and tries to do things with them regularly. Many of the older children turn to her as a sympathetic listener and advisor. Every weekend she rides a church bus to a nearby town with neighborhood children. She provides supervision for these children, many of whose parents would not let them go so far away without a responsible adult friend. She occasionally meets with some other women in the neighborhood to talk about personal problems and personal goals. She is working with Mrs. P. to develop a summer youth work program.

One single young Mexican man, Mr. R., provides tutoring to high school students. He is also actively seeking to develop and improve the Mexican community. Another Mexican man provides people with transportation, helps them find jobs and refers people to the appropriate resources. Mr. S., an older black man, visits the elderly in the community, goes with people on agency visits, and talks to parents about children. He has recently helped to bring together a small group of elderly neighbors who would like to socialize and take recreational trips together.

[Case No. 25]

Sometimes the help provided by informal helpers is not so explicitly recognized as was the case in the examples above. Even so, the help provided can make a great difference even in cases where problems may be severe. The following example illustrates informal helping activities that played an important role in sustaining a mentally ill individual in a small rural town:

When she was observing the village square, Janice had noticed a middle-aged woman, obviously seriously mentally disturbed, bizarre in appearance, and talking and gesturing to herself. It seemed only a question of time before she would come to official notice and be sent to a mental hospital or, if her habits exhausted the patience of her small personal commercial unpaid network, to the sheriff's office. In a larger place she might well drop out of sight and be "lost in the gutter." She made the same round of calls every morning—a stop at the barber shop, at the tavern and then on to the post office. Janice learned that she had the barber cut a small square of hair just above her hairline daily because it kept down "the voices"; that the soda water the tavern keeper gave her also had this effect to the extent that she could then go and mingle with the other women at the post office. Somehow, she learned of the expanded activities of a public health nurse whom she had not previously contacted. Now, when she ran out of money toward the end of the month and faced eviction from her hotel room she would go to the nurse who would enlist the help of several ministers to tide her over.

[*Case No. 20*]

There are also informal helpers who play key roles in the lives of quite a number of individuals with difficult problems. The scope of their helping activities spans a wide range of functions that are often provided by formal services. An example from a midwestern urban community highlights the role of an owner of a single room occupancy hotel. The hotel houses approximately seventy male and female residents who range in age from early twenties to late seventies:

The owner set about restoring the hotel to its original grandeur—by stripping paint to reveal an old oak staircase, for example, and affixing a brass name-plate on the front door. He also decided to continue to offer low-cost rentals to marginal individuals in the area, and was concerned, as well, with assuring that the seventy residents of the hotel received any and all of the services due them. To this end he invited the participation of a team of staff from Public Health, Mental Health and Social Services. This team meets weekly with the owner to discuss the needs of the various residents, provides a screening function (weeding out anyone who is known to be violent); and assures his residents direct access to the full range of services and social supports available in the local area. He personally looks out for the residents, all of whom are financially marginal and many of whom are aftercare, public welfare, or SSI recipients; he provides refreshments for an informal social hour once a week, inviting all the residents to come and mingle, to chat with him or with each other. At the end of the month when pocketbooks are thin he informs his residents of free meals available in the area; on some holidays he provides a turkey dinner for the residents, which they can eat together or take back to their own rooms.

[*Case No. 23*]

These examples illustrate that informal helping can be viewed broadly as a complex matter influenced by the setting, the attributes of the helper involved, and the nature of the relationships among those providing and receiving help. Many times the specific acts of help are not even perceived as such but rather seen as part of everyday living. The case illustrations also show the varying degrees of responsibility that different helpers assume in dealing with a given problem or individual. Some helpers, such as the people who helped the mentally ill woman, play limited roles, while others, such as the owner of the single room occupancy hotel, take on a great deal of responsibility.

Informal Helping: What Influences Its Form?

Our study did not specifically address the issue of the motives underlying helpful acts; whether all helpful action can be explained in terms of receiving or expecting something in return for the action or whether purely altruistic acts occur. Notwithstanding this basic controversy, it is clear that helping is influenced and directed by a variety of social factors. Studies of volunteerism, charitable behavior, aid given in emergency situations or between strangers as well as other forms of "prosocial behavior" (Wispe, 1972), suggest that there are essentially four major ways of cataloging the influences on informal helping. Generally speaking, helping may stem from, and take particular forms based on, cultural traditions, developmental experiences and learned behavior, the influence of general social norms, or, finally the rules that govern interpersonal exchange. These factors are all mentioned by informal helpers when asked, "Why do you help?" In addition, they exert an influence on whether or not helping occurs in a specific situation, who helps and is helped, and what kind of help is offered. Each of these four sources of influence can be illustrated with examples of informal helping found within our sample of thirty agencies.

THE INFLUENCE OF TRADITION

Looked at in very broad terms, the dynamics of informal helping are influenced by long-standing cultural patterns of rights and responsibilities that characterize groups that differ in ethnicity, religion, social class, or local tradition. Several examples of the influence of traditional values are found among the programs in our study. In one program serving the elderly, the ethnic traditions limited who was considered "appropriate" to help:

There is a clear split between the Mexican-American and Anglo populations within the barrio that has led to problems in the exchange of help. Until recently all of the helpers were Mexican-American, and they did not define the Anglos, who lived in larger and nicer houses, as being in need of aid. They are also reluctant to aid those who have children in the city; the family norms are very strong and it is argued that it is the children's responsibility to help their elderly parents.
[*Case No. 9*]

Another program concerned with promoting informal helping in a rural community in Pennsylvania encountered local traditions that limited the range of help that was considered appropriate:

While one might expect the more rural county to be more cohesive, a local minister characterized the people as not getting together often, even though they all know each other. While they will pitch in to help during a crisis, open communication and expression of feelings are not the norm. The usual response to someone coming for help, he says, is to give them practical, concrete advice, and terse advice at that: "If you need money, you either work hard or you go to a bank and borrow it"; "If your husband is running around, you better make things better at home for him."
[*Case No. 22*]

The influence of tradition is sometimes a strength rather than a hindrance to certain types of helping. Several agencies found that strong ties among residents, church groups, and cultural traditions were forces promoting helping and relied on these traditions to reinforce existing patterns and to make new programs acceptable. For example, one program promoting self-help within an ethnic community found that basing aid on religious traditions could surmount the initial distrust of program efforts:

> *There has been* some distrust of a program which offers aid without seeming to expect anything tangible in return. Some wondered, "What's the catch?" The most successful approach to communicating and instilling the concept of mutual aid has been to tie the concept to Christian principles: "What you do for the least of my brothers, you do for me."
>
> [*Case No. 9*]

People often give religious principles as a personal reason for helping whether or not they are part of an organized religious group: "It's the Christian thing to do," or "My religion says I should help." One program director noted, "The church is the dominant organization in the rural area. . . . People who are prominent in that kind of organization are very often the same people who people go to in general" (Salber, 1975).

THE INFLUENCE OF LEARNING

An individual's family background and prior experience are also important in shaping helpful behavior (Cochran & Brassard, 1979; Kanfer, 1979). Acts of helping can be learned, reinforced, or changed in the course of individual development. Prior research in this area has looked at the influence of individual factors such as age, sex, education, and family background as well as situational factors such as the presence of role models in shaping the willingness and ability of a person to provide certain types of help and assistance (Bryan, 1972; Rosenhan, 1972). The general weight of evidence suggests, very simply, that when a person has had opportunities to help and the experience has been positive, they are likely to continue to help. The presence of other people who may serve as role models for helping behavior may sensitize a person to a particular problem, indicate behaviors that may be helpful, and offer a chance for an individual to weigh the costs and benefits associated with helping. Role models may be other family members, peers who share common concerns, and others with whom a person has a significant relationship.

Family background is frequently cited by people who are asked why they help others. Speaking of natural helpers, one project director said "Sometimes [they help] because their mothers were that kind of person and they grew up in a household where people asked their advice." Another helper said, "Mom and Dad always helped people."

The influence of learning also exerts itself in instances where people are motivated to share similar solutions with those who have similar problems. When people are at the same stage in dealing with a problem, the learning is based on mutual exploration of the problem where frustrations, insights, and solutions are shared in a give and take process. The following example of discussion groups for parents of infants illustrates this model:

> *The groups that* the program works with bring together mothers of newborns that live within a loosely defined common neighborhood. Occasionally these young mothers have had prior contacts in prenatal classes, school, or churches. In most instances they have not. Some of the women also invite other friends with young children so that personal ties are not excluded. However, through the group meetings, a locality-based support network develops. Although staff members are instrumental in bringing the groups of new mothers together, and initially act as facilitators or catalysts for group activities, most groups soon take control of their own structure and activities. Even those who are at first skeptical or reluctant often come to find the meeting beneficial. Sharing the joys and difficulties of raising small children leads to new friendships and supports and the group becomes a way of helping each other learn to be better parents.
>
> [*Case No. 10*]

Some people would like to help others with similar problems in order to share what they have learned "the hard way," in the process of solving their own problems. One program working to promote the adjustment of parents of developmentally disabled children illustrates this motivation:

> *Parents who have* just found out that their child is retarded and are wondering what it will be like to raise a handicapped child are

introduced to parents who have been through the same experience. The parents come from all parts of the county and all socioeconomic levels. Without a common meeting ground they would not be likely to become acquainted. Once they are, they may establish some other ties and some have even become good friends but, in general, the relationship is confined to the mutual concern of parenting a retarded child.

Once a parent becomes known as a helper, that person may begin to get requests for help from their own network of friends, relatives and acquaintances. For example, one parent is a nurse and gets a number of direct referrals from her professional connections. The exchange that occurs between the experienced parents and parents who request help is described by one parent as going through three phases: "Uppermost is talking about the child. They want to know all about my child and then they talk about theirs. The second thing is the emotional. What they went through when they were told. Then they finally get to services, the future. I do a lot of listening and offer suggestions and support."

[*Case No. 17*]

This particular example also highlights how helping based on learning shifts and changes for individuals over the course of their development. As concerns and experiences change, so does the process of providing or receiving help:

There seems to be a period of readiness to help. It comes after the parent has fully accepted the fact that the child is retarded and has learned about services. The parent is then eager to meet new parents and help them. After a while, however, usually by the time the child is school age, the parent no longer feels close to the experience of a new parent and is interested in other issues of more immediate concern, such as advocating for more services from the school system and planning for the child's future as an adult.

There may also be a point of readiness for a new parent. The social worker recalled one family that a worker at one of the large rehabilitation agencies had told her about. The worker said she told the mother about the parent's group and suggested she contact them several times but the mother never seemed to pay much attention. Then one day the mother said, "Why didn't you ever tell me about the program? My friend told me about it and I really would have liked to know about it sooner." Another mother who is now a parent helper recalled that her doctor suggested several times while she was still in the hospital that she call another patient who also had a child with Downs Syndrome. She resisted the suggestion until she was home and the realities of caring for the child were really becoming apparent. She then called the mother. Now she says, "I wish I had called her sooner, it would have saved me days of grief."

[*Case No. 17*]

THE INFLUENCE OF NORMS

Another way of looking at informal helping emphasizes the influence of generally shared social norms which establish certain expectations of people to provide help or to take responsibility for others and which are reinforced by social approval (Staub, 1972). Research in this area has looked at how people individualize social norms through experience and at how differences in the specific situation influence the likelihood of helping. A major element of this orientation is concerned with situations in which no help is given because responsibility is so diffuse that no one person feels the pressure of social expectations to provide help. Having others aware that one is being helpful tends to motivate conformance to norms of social responsibility.

There are several examples of helping activities among the programs in our study where the influence of social norms appears to operate. The clearest examples of helping activities influenced by social norms come from programs involving caregivers of dependent family members where the norm of "taking care of one's own" is evoked. This type of motivation seemed particularly obvious in a New York program in midtown Manhattan that is working with the caregivers of the elderly. The agency had conducted a survey of caregivers:

Among their clients, 54 percent of the primary caregivers were children of the aging person, 25 percent were spouses, and 10 percent siblings. Of the elderly, 72 percent were female, with the most common caregiver being the daughter. The evidence also indicates that if the son is the primary caregiver, his wife is usually also very involved in caregiving. On the other hand, the daughter often tries to look after the older parent without involving her husband or children at all, even trying to hide her responsibilities from the family. Siblings, on the other hand, are expected to share equally in caregiving but rarely do. The caregivers themselves range widely in their involvement in the role, based largely on the needs of the older person. Some may only visit a few times a week or do grocery shopping, while others may be involved in 24-hour care of a senile or severely physically disabled person. The caregiver tends to live near the aging relative, with about half sharing a residence (more than half of these are spouses). An additional 14 percent live in the same building, and only 7 percent live more than an hour away.

The study also provides insight into the motivation for becoming a caregiver. For those children with a long-term close relationship with the parent, love may be a major reason for helping. Many of the parent-child relationships had been characterized by conflict for years; however, in these cases motivation included a feeling of family responsibility, reciprocation for help received in the past, a sense of personal satisfaction, filling a void in their own lives, and avoiding nursing home placement at all costs. The ability to cope with the caregiver role was harder for those with a history of conflict, and also for those with nuclear families of their own.

[Case No. 4]

The data from this agency show how the influence of the social responsibility norm can be mediated by such factors as the degree of dependency of the elderly family member, prior experiences, and physical proximity between the caregiver and the elderly family member, all of which affected the likelihood that a potential caregiver would take responsibility. These factors have also emerged from other research as important in determining the degree of influence of normative expectations (Berkowitz, 1972).

Agency staff can increase helping efforts by providing social approval, as illustrated by a program promoting neighborhood helping in the course of providing community development services:

Some individuals occupied a more "middle of the road" position when they were first encountered. They helped some and had lived in a neighborhood for a long time, but had not yet come to perform a major helping role. For this type, the recognition the program provided motivated them to assume a greater responsibility for helping in their neighborhood. For example, an elderly woman who had rented a house in the area for some fifteen years seemed to take the attitude that being "chosen" for the program gave her a legitimacy in helping others. Whereas before she might have been reluctant to get actively involved, the program motivated her to become more assertive in helping a wider range of people in her neighborhood. Now, she monitors neighborhood activity, makes frequent visits to several older residents in the neighborhood to check on how they are doing, and helps others who need formal assistance to obtain services.

[Case No. 26]

THE INFLUENCE OF EXCHANGE

Theories of social exchange which incorporate such concepts as reciprocity, indebtedness, equity, and justice probably explain the most prevalent forms of informal helping activities observed in our study (Adams, 1965; Gouldner, 1960; Greenberg, 1976; Homans, 1961; Thibaut & Kelley, 1959). Exchange theory provides a more utilitarian view of helping activities by examining the balance of personal or social costs and benefits involved in the interaction between those providing and those receiving help. In this view, a person helps because of an expectation of future rewards or in order to repay a debt resulting from having been helped before. Notions such as indebtedness, justice, and compensation are used to refer to the obligation an individual feels to provide help. This obligation is contingent on a number of factors:

> The intensity of the recipient's need at the time the benefit was bestowed ("a friend in need . . ."), the resources of the donor ("he gave although he could ill afford it"), the motives imputed to the donor ("without thought of gain"), and the nature of the constraints which are perceived to exist or to be absent ("he gave of his own free will . . .") [Gouldner, 1960:171].

The concept of *reciprocity* can be used to denote an exchange relationship in which the expectation is that a favor must be repaid in equal value to the donor by the recipient. Such exchange need not balance out over the short term; some relationships such as that between parent and child may involve very long-term exchanges. When a group of individuals interact or when relationships are more intimate or long-standing, an expectation of *mutuality* may prevail in which a favor given may be repaid by helping someone else with the idea that, over time, things will balance out.

Reciprocity and mutuality serve as motivating factors in many of the programs observed in our study. Reciprocity was particularly common in neighborhood situations as was seen in a program serving the elderly in a neighborhood with long-term residents:

> *People in the area* seemed willing to both give and receive help from their neighbors. They generally preferred to reciprocate in some way if they could and the staff sometimes found ways to help them do so. For example, a man who needed help with mowing his lawn arranged to

have the young man next door mow his lawn in exchange for being allowed to borrow the older man's mower.

[*Case No. 2*]

Mutuality can also occur within a neighborhood setting but more often appears when people have come together out of common concern. For example, one program had organized a group of recently widowed persons within a neighborhood area:

Within the younger widows group, other more instrumental exchanges also took place as well—some of the women helped widowers with meal planning and cooking skills, while the men did home repairs or took the kids fishing. Such exchanges were at an informal level that involved local norms of mutuality: "I'll help you if you need it, because somebody helped me when I was in need."

[*Case No. 28*]

Sometimes the expectation of reciprocity can create strains in a helping relationship, particularly when one party is unable to reciprocate because of a lack of resources or physical limitations. This was observed in programs serving the frail elderly, as the following example illustrates:

Often, an elderly client will want to "repay the favor" but may only be able to do so by offering money which is usually refused by the helpers. In some ways both the helper and the client are in a "double bind" if the relationship is to continue to be based on mutual concern. The helper can't accept payment for helping but the elderly client often is unable to offer other things in return. Many times this results in the elderly individual seeking formal services because of their feeling of violating the norm of reciprocity in a peer relationship. Sometimes the situation can be improved by involving a youth to do yard work or household chores for payment, where the idea of reciprocity is viewed differently.

[*Case No. 7*]

Finally, another example illustrates how one program fostered the expectation of mutuality in order to promote informal helping activities:

One very active helper now is always available for friendly visits and makes a point of visiting others when in the hospital. The staff first knew him as an extremely shy man who frequented the nutrition center. When he had a heart attack, they visited him at the hospital, and this convinced him that they really did care about him. He shows his gratitude by passing on this caring to others.

[*Case No. 9*]

The four major influences on the form helping may take—norms, tradition, personal development, and exchange—are not mutually exclusive in their action. Rather, a person feels and responds to a multitude of influences, although one type of influence may be particularly compelling depending on the nature of what that person perceives as needed by another and what is judged to be appropriate. Each suggests ways in which formal services can act to increase the likelihood that informal help will be provided.

Types of Informal Helpers

The kinds of help that people provide and the various influences that shape or direct different helping activities indicate the pluralistic nature of informal helping networks. This diversity can also be seen by examining the variety of roles played by different individuals who compose a given helping network. For example, helpers in ongoing networks of relationships include family members, trusted friends, and new acquaintances willing to help out. People may offer to help strangers as volunteers or members of a mutual aid group because they have a special concern for particular problems they have experienced in their own lives, want to try out a role analogous to a professional helping role, or have time and skills that are underutilized. Neighborhood or community helpers may have some special talent, be particularly resourceful in getting things done, or simply take an interest in local concerns and get involved with a wide range of others. These different types of people perform a variety of essential roles as part of a helping network for others. Some are specialists in the sense that they have a particular knowledge or skill that is well suited to specific tasks. Others are generalists and help out in multiple ways. For many, what they do is an integral part of their lives and may be a consequence of family background, a particular job or position, or other personal experience.

Among the agencies in our study, we were able to classify the variety of helping roles into six basic types of helpers. These are family and friends, neighbors, natural helpers, role-related helpers, people with similar problems, and volunteers. We discuss each of these types of helpers separately below, but it should be emphasized that these six types are best seen as activities or roles rather than types of people. For example, the same woman may be actively involved in supporting an elderly parent *(family and friends)*, part of a cooperative day care exchange *(similar problems)*, and a volunteer in a socialization program for ex-patients *(volunteer)*. Since helping may result from interest in a particular problem and may take different forms over time, the types are not static, either. Parents of a retarded child may belong to a support group when their child is an infant, then volunteer in a special preschool program, and later become active in an association advocating the establishment of more group homes for retarded adults as their child's needs change.

In order to provide an overview of the six types of informal helpers, Tables 2.1 and 2.2 provide a profile of a variety of attributes associated with each type. In Table 2.1, the personal attributes of the helper refer to the attributes that the agency focuses on in identifying or selecting informal helpers. The target populations are those which were the primary focus of the efforts of the agency. Table 2.2 presents a number of characteristics of the kind of help being provided and relates them to the type of helper. The helping activities were identified from content analysis; the four sets of activities shown represent the four factors that emerged from factor analysis of a more inclusive set of helping activities. Scores are used to reflect whether a given attribute rates high (++), medium (+) or low (0) in characterizing a particular helper type, with significant differences among helper types shown by asterisks after the relevant attribute. Each helper type will be discussed drawing from the profiles of attributes, relevant literature and examples from case studies of the agencies.

Family and Friends. Despite the fact that family and friends are the most intimate and ubiquitous sources of help for all but the most isolated individuals (Sussman, 1965; Wellman, 1979), few service agencies have developed conscious, well thought out ways of interacting with this form of helping. Among the family and friends, helping was generally based on commitment and motivation to help rather than on special skills or knowledge. Yet, they were offering substantial assistance, ranging from socializing and checking in to see that everything was all right to home maintenance or intensive

TABLE 2.1 Helper and Recipient Characteristics

	Family and Friends	Neighbors	Helper Type Natural Helpers	Role-Related Helpers	People with Similar Problems	Volunteers
n^a	7	13	4	7	21	8
Sex of Helper (% Female)*	41-60	41-60	41-60	21-40	41-60	61-80
Personal Attributes						
Leadership in networks*	0	+	++	++	0	0
Helping skills	+	+	++	+	0	+
Motivation*	++	+	++	++	+	++
Shared experience*	0	0	+	0	++	0
Special knowledge	0	0	0	+	0	+
Target Population						
Elderly	4	5	1	3	6	1
Mental health	2	3	1	1	6	2
Disabled	0	0	0	0	4	3
Families	1	0	0	0	5	2
General community	0	5	2	3	0	0
Status Relationship—Helper and Recipient						
Helpers higher in SES*	+	+	+	+	0	++
Helpers have same life situation, problems*	0	+	+	0	++	0
Helpers cope better with problems	++	+	++	+	+	++

Note: The notations "0", "+", and "++" indicate the range into which the mean score falls. Specifically, ++ = M > 3.0; + = M between 2.0 and 2.9; 0 = M < 2.0 on a scale ranging from 4 = "very typical" to 1 = "not at all typical".
a. Numbers indicate the number of approaches, out of the total of 60 program approaches which were predominantly working with the particular type of helper.
* indicates one-way ANOVA, p < .01.

TABLE 2.2 Helping Activities

	Helper Type					
n^a	Family and Friends 7	Neighbors 13	Natural Helpers 4	Role-Related Helpers 7	People with Similar Problems 21	Volunteers 8
Kind of Network Worked With						
Individual client (not part of their personal network)*	0	0	0	+	0	++
Personal networks of neighbors, friends, family*	++	+	++	0	0	0
Peer group, mutual aid or common interest*	0	0	+	0	++	0
Locality-based*	0	++	++	+	+	0
Length of Relationship*	long-term	moderately long	long-term*	moderately long	moderately long	moderately long
Helping Activities						
Caretaking (material assistance, services, money)	+	+	+	+	0	0
Joint action (cooperative communal activity, organizing, advocacy, planning)*	0	0	++	+	+	0
Friendship (association, emotional support)*	++	+	++	0	++	+
Problem-solving (cognitive guidance, linking)	+	+	++	+	+	++
Reciprocity (returns to helper)						
Tangible over short-term	0	0	0	0	+	0
Tangible over long-term	++	++	++	0	0	0
Pass along to others	+	++	++	++	+	0
Expected part of helping roles*	0	+	++	++	0	++
No expectations of reward	+	+	++	++	+	+
Rewards external to relationship needed*	0				0	+
Number of People Helped per Helper*	one	many	many	many	no designated helpers and helpees	several

Note: The notations "0", "+" and "++" indicate the range into which the mean score falls. Specifically ++ = M > 3.0; + = M between 2.0 and 2.9; 0 = M < 2.0 on a scale ranging from 4 = "very typical" to 1 = "not at all typical".

a. Numbers indicate the number of approaches, out of the total of 60 program approaches which were predominantly working with the particular type of helper.

* indicates one-way ANOVA, p < .01.

47

home nursing care. They were also important sources of advice and information about services.

Neighbors. The concept of neighbors or neighborhood, as we discuss in Chapter 7, is often ambiguous because it can refer to several different levels of social organization (Keller, 1968). For many people, the neighborhood is seen as primarily their own block; on this block are the neighbors they know personally with whom they are most likely to exchange help. While some neighbors may come to be defined as friends, in general the relationship combines a high level of knowledge about many aspects of one another's lives with a fairly low level of involvement (Keller, 1968). Compared to family and friends, there are generally more defined limits on the forms of helping that are appropriate to ask for and offer (Litwak, 1978). The ability of the neighbor to be helpful is based on accessibility and willingness rather than on having special skills or similar experiences. Using the small-scale definition of the neighborhood, neighbors can be particularly important in helping the elderly.

Where the agency was working with a larger-scale neighborhood, the role of the neighbor changed from one-to-one exchanges to advocacy or participation in group efforts intended to benefit the neighborhood as a whole rather than specific neighbors. However, a side effect of such group action is often the fostering of new individual relationships among neighbors.

Natural Helpers. While we are almost all involved in helping and receiving help from others, there are some people for whom this is a more central role in their lives, or who are simply better at it than most of us. They are individuals turned to by many others for aid and advice, either for general problems or for specific areas in which they are felt to have expertise. These are the people we have termed natural helpers or central figures (Collins & Pancoast, 1976). For the natural helpers in our sample, helping was less based on the mutuality of neighboring or the obligations of kinship or long-standing friendship and more on personal motivation to help others and on natural helping skills which earned them the respect and confidence of those with whom they interacted.

Some natural helpers held positions of community leadership. For example, one natural helper in a small New England town was elected president of the Senior Council. In addition to her official duties, this position enabled her to extend her helping activities to more of the town's elderly and to adult children who were primary caregivers for their elderly parents. Other natural helpers prefer to confine their helping activities to a circle of relatives, friends, and neighbors. One such natural helper provided free car repair services while at the same time teaching teenagers how to fix cars. Another was described by a worker in one of the programs as "the Play Lady," a natural helper who liked children and did things for them— trips, parties, projects—with the agency helping to cover her costs. Often such a helper has children of her own and includes neighborhood children in her outings with her own children.

Members of the natural helper's network are usually aware that the helpers are exceptional people. One helper said, "My husband calls me the community mother" but she, like many helpers, denied that she was doing anything extraordinary (see also Snyder, 1976). These helpers tend to have long-term relationships with those they help and with the agency. They usually are of the same socioeconomic status as those they help and have similar problems, but they exhibit superior coping abilities.

Role-Related Helpers. While these people may also have the interpersonal skills that are typical of the natural helper, they come to the attention of the agency because of influential roles they fill in the community, sometimes as a gatekeeper, sometimes as an opinion leader. Some fill roles, such as a minister or public health nurse, that are considered helping roles. Others have positions that locate them at crossroads where they are likely to be turned to for help because of their visibility. These include storekeepers, postmasters, teachers, and managers of residential hotels.

Within our sample, role-related helpers often helped others indirectly by being active on agency-sponsored task forces or in the general community. Some provided help to people directly: a postmistress in a small town who allowed the post office to become the main social center; a pharmacist who helped older people pay their bills and always had a pot of coffee on; and a fundamentalist minister on an Indian reservation who developed a youth center within the church and was one of the primary sources of transportation for an isolated community.

This is the only category of helper in which men were in the majority, perhaps because most of the occupations involved are largely filled by men. Within their occupationally defined helping role, they were less likely to provide friendship and emotional support than advice, referral, and some services.

People with Similar Problems. The most prevalent type of helping we found in our sample was that from people with similar problems, although research indicates that it is not the most common form of helping in the general population (Lieberman & Mullan, 1978). A survey in California (Field Research Corporation, 1979) found that while 39 percent of those interviewed confided in a friend in times of emotional stress, only 9 percent sought out others with similar problems. Since our study was based on informal helpers who were known to and involved with formal services agencies, the relatively large number of mutual aid activities we observed probably reflects the greater attention which professionals have paid to this form of helping than to the other types.

In some ways, this is the most "artificial" form of helping described here in that it is the only form which seldom occurred in the homes of those involved and in which short-term returns were expected by the participants. Helpers with similar problems sometimes helped each other within the context of self-help groups, including groups for abused women, widows, caregivers to the elderly, and parents of young children. Casual drop-in contact fostered by a senior center or a program providing temporary child care was another basis for mutual aid. The one-to-one relationship was a third type, as when parents of mentally retarded children were matched with parents who had just found out their child was retarded and provided support and information on a family-to-family basis. In another instance, a physically disabled person who was good at repairing wheelchairs taught the skill to other disabled persons.

Much of the interaction within such groups in our sample involved friendship and the pleasures of associating with similar people as much as the resolution of problems. The participants needed no prior experience in helping others and their ongoing relationships with others were not important to the helping process. While shared experience was the main qualification for helpfulness, often this arose from shared status rather than common problems. For example, being old or having young children gave people something in common but was not perceived as a "problem."

Volunteers. Volunteers are probably the most familiar type of informal helper to most professionals. This form of help is usually stranger-to-stranger and channeled through a formal organization. Of all the forms of helping described here, it is most likely to involve inequality of status between the helper and recipient—both in terms of socioeconomic status and general coping ability. There is also an unequal exchange relationship, with the volunteer clearly defined as the helper. While a mutual relationship may develop, and indeed was often encouraged by these agencies, it is not usually part of the standard volunteer role. Because there is already a rich body of literature on volunteerism, we chose only examples in which the volunteers were encouraged by the agency to be as "natural" as possible—to use their personal skills and networks on behalf of a client or group of clients and to develop a relationship based, as far as possible, on the model of naturally occurring friendship.

This was the only type of help in which women predominated, probably reflecting the greater numbers of women who have time for extensive volunteer activities. Motivation in terms of willingness to help and concern for problems was a more important personal characteristic than helping skills or ongoing relationships. Problem-solving was the most common helping activity. Volunteers were involved with a wide range of problems and target populations.

Embedded and Created Helping Relationships

Perhaps one of the fundamental differences in the character of informal helping hinges on whether help is exchanged between those who have an existing relationship or involves people whose relationships were initiated by an agency. Family and friends, neighbors, natural helpers, and role-related helpers involve helping relationships that are *embedded* in ongoing networks of relationships among people who share other bases for relating: kinship, residential proximity, membership in clubs or churches, or patronage of the same stores and institutions. People with similar problems and volunteers have helping relationships that are *created*, usually by a formal agency to meet a specific need. Often they represent attempts by the agencies to develop an informal helping system for people or problems for whom existing systems either do not exist or are not effective. This distinction has major implications for the kind of help exchanged, the reasons underlying the provision of help, and the types of helpers that may be involved.

There are a number of contrasts between the two categories of helping relationships that are important for professionals to understand if they are to work productively with both types. In many ways, the strengths of one category of helping are the weaknesses of the other.

Embedded helping relationships are likely to be meeting basic needs—material assistance, health care, protective services—and to be long-term relationships with a heavy investment of time, responsibility, and concern. They require few agency resources to initiate or maintain. They are highly individualized and sensitive to the preferences of the participants. They are extremely flexible, reflecting what Diana Trilling has called "the endless improvisation of mutuality" (Harlow, 1979:48).

On the other hand, embedded relationships help fewer people per helper. They are dependent on existing relationships and therefore on opportunities for such relationships to develop. Although we found such helpers in every kind of setting from the most rural to the most urban, some would argue that the opportunities for developing and sustaining such relationships are lessening due to geographic mobility, changes in family size and structure, and new work roles for women. In addition, the embedded helping relationship is affected by the other relationships in the network and by the values, mores, and knowledge of the participants. Help may be given only to certain favored persons (e.g., of the same race or religion) or heavy conditions may be attached. Because the relationships are idiosyncratic, agencies which want to relate to them must be willing to be very flexible and to spend some time at the outset identifying the helpers and understanding the culture of the particular network or neighborhood.

Created relationships present the opportunity for people to develop new helping roles, skills, and values. This makes them especially useful for people who are isolated and lack flourishing networks. Their initiation can be directed by the agency and hence can be better targeted on the needs and clients the agency is most concerned to serve. They are also more specialized and therefore more compatible with specialized formal services. They are more open and egalitarian than embedded relationships in the sense that a willingness to help or participate is the only requirement for helper status. This type of helping is relatively easy for agencies to work with since helpers can be recruited by advertisement, referral, or from the client group.

Created helping relationships also have drawbacks, however. They require a fairly heavy investment of agency resources in order to initiate and sustain them. The helping relationships tend to be shorter in duration than embedded ones and involve fewer basic services and more short-term problem solving. The agency is probably more able to impose a created helping relationship on a recipient. This may have negative consequences for the person being helped who may find the relationship less satisfactory than one they have initiated and feel they have either "earned" by past services or can repay at a future time. As R. A. Parker (1980:21) has said, "If one turns to the recipients of tending services it is instructive to consider what kinds of terms they are prepared to accept for *being* helped. In some ways acts of giving are less problematic than acts of receiving."

Conclusion

We began by asking the question: "What can be expected of informal sources of help for problems requiring formal services?" Very simply, the answer is quite a bit. At different times, for different reasons, and in different situations, informal helpers provide a wide range of assistance from tangible things such as food, housing, and money to intangibles such as emotional support, practical advice, and personal influence. Informal helpers deal with problems at all levels of severity. We have found that there are a variety of factors which influence helping and which shape the kind of contribution that will be made and the degree of responsibility that will be assumed. Further, we have also seen that different types of helpers have different characteristics and varying needs for support from professionals.

The major lesson to be gleaned from our discussion is that the value of informal sources of helping in dealing with a given problem depends as much on the appropriateness of the opportunities presented for providing help as it does on the characteristics of the helpers. Helpers are made as well as born. The task for agencies lies in finding ways to shape, enhance, and maintain incentives for informal helping behaviors by understanding what may be necessary given the requirements of different problems, situational constraints, and types of helpers. Attempting to invoke the influence of local traditions where there are none or emphasizing the norm of social responsibility among strangers or in situations that may create undue burden for an individual are instances in which the incentives provided do not match the task required. Promoting mutuality among people who have the same problems or experiences and reciprocity among neighbors exemplify approaches that are more appropriate. This is not to suggest that there are hard and fast guidelines for eliciting and sustaining informal helping, but rather to emphasize that opportunities for helping have to be individualized, open, and flexible.

Chapter 3

PROFESSIONAL PARTNERSHIPS WITH INFORMAL HELPERS

Social welfare services have come a long way from their beginnings in the Charity Organization Societies and the Settlement House movement, when the vast bulk of service work was done by "volunteers." Despite some recognized shortcomings and inadequacies in formal services, bureaucratically organized, professional services have come to be an accepted part of modern society. In the context of today's large, complex social welfare system, agency administrators and direct service workers have to make a conscious and deliberate effort to see beyond the services which are in place, rearticulate a philosophy of how services are to be given, and reach out to the community in new, tentative, and exploratory ways.

Reviewing the work of the agencies in our sample, there is a sense that human services have come full circle, reaching back to the beginnings of organized human services to find the basis for a renewed partnership with people who are helping one another in their everyday lives. This rekindling of tradition is illustrated by the surprising degree of similarity in the philosophical rationales developed by agency staff to conceptualize their work with informal helping networks. This shared philosophy emphasizes the principles of self-determination, self-reliance, and mutual aid, which serve as a frame of reference for staff in providing help. In working with clients, this may involve looking at an individual's abilities and strengths, seeing how people may be helped by others or help themselves, being concerned to have people take responsibility for the help they receive, and identifying ways for individuals who share problems to also share solutions. In working with the community, staff may express a more political conception of helping by helping the community recognize and mobilize its own strengths and resources, emphasizing community control over programs, and advocating for individual rights. Throughout, there is a belief that "people do best when they're in charge." It is this belief that directs staff to look at natural support networks, self-help efforts, and informal helpers in their work.

To accomplish this, staff often conceptualize their task as strengthening informal helping activities and enlarging the channels of access to formal services. They develop staff roles that serve as "bridges" between formal and informal systems. The building blocks of these roles are an appreciation of the social connections among people in the community and a realization that the world of informal caring has its own rules and norms that must be respected.

Opportunities for Developing Linkages

Each program in the study offered a unique blend of formal and informal ways of helping people. The types of problems and client populations the agency worked with, the stability of the neighborhood or community in which clients lived, the legal and political climate encountered by the agency, the agency's organizational base, and the personalities of the staff and informal helpers all served to influence the directions pursued in linking the efforts of professional staff and informal helpers. Table 3.1 presents examples of types of linkages that were observed among the thirty agencies, as they varied by target population and the specific problems addressed.

The kind of helping networks that staff establish links with depends both on the problem and the objectives of concern to an agency. The reasons staff have for seeking out informal sources of help are major influences in the way staff define and identify a helping network. Several patterns are shown in Table 3.1. Some agencies focus exclusively on a given client (e.g., an elderly widow), and are concerned with identifying the *personal support* network of that individual. Staff may draw upon outside support resources when the existing personal network of a client is limited or not supportive.

TABLE 3.1 Opportunities for Developing Linkages

TARGET POPULATIONS

Problem Focus	Elderly	Children, Youth and Families	Developmental and Physical Disabled	Mental Health Clients	Low Income and Ethnic Communities
Individual rights • access to services • acceptability and appropriateness of services • stigmatizing problems	• organize elder forum to identify needs and local resources • establish linkages between elderly groups in low income housing and local Commissions on Aging	• develop parent advising board to participate in youth and children's services • establish youth advisory board to provide input to elected officials on youth concerns	• establish Parent Advocates groups to lobby for educational rights for developmentally disabled children • establish consumer coalition for disabled to advocate for transportation accessibility, curbcuts, barrier free housing	• develop pool of volunteer citizens to help obtain services for returning mental hospital patients • organize consumer corporation to advocate for mentally ill • act as advisor to client self-help group	• establish constituency groups among providers, consumers, opinion leaders to identify local resources and organize services • organize and charter Neighborhood Planning Council to approve or initiate local economic development
Needs for material assistance • food, housing • jobs	• recruit local residents to help in home repair for elderly • support neighborhood helpers who provide home aid • contact stores, banks, to improve service to elderly	• foster mutual aid network among abused women to develop cooperative living arrangement • develop network of families in communities to provide temporary shelter care for runaway youth • use lay therapists to act as advocates to ensure that abusive families' basic material needs are met	• establish cooperative living arrangements among severely disabled • develop parents group to assist retarded adults to find jobs	• establish citizen/consumer partnership to organize employment and housing opportunities for chronic mental patients • consult with SRO and boarding home managers to improve living situations of chronic patients	• establish mutual aid groups among unemployed persons to exchange information about job search strategies • develop self-help "tools and skills bank" to assist in rehabilitating housing • establish neighborhood cooperative to fund local development and provide jobs

(Continued)

57

TABLE 3.1 Opportunities for Developing Linkages (continued)

Problem Focus	Elderly	TARGET POPULATIONS Children, Youth and Families	Developmental and Physical Disabled	Mental Health Clients	Low Income and Ethnic Communities
Needs for social and emotional support • limitations in social skills • assistance with activities of daily living	• enlist natural helper in neighborhoods to provide friendly visiting • develop neighborhood based peer support groups to increase mutual aid	• recruit and train lay helpers to provide compassionate support to identified child abuse parents • develop mutual aid groups among single parent families • develop mutual aid group among widow(er)s with dependent children	• develop links between parents of disabled children to provide support and advice on raising child • consult with and promote self-help groups among retarded, e.g., People First	• develop community networks among ex-patients to initiate and plan social and recreational activities • develop mutual aid groups for patients • develop mutual aid group and peer telephone network among agoraphobics	• recruit and train natural helpers to provide informal helping to residents • facilitate neighborhood support among residents
Multiple problems • chronic problem • family burden	• develop support groups for adult children of frail elderly • provide support services to family members to sustain the existing help provided • enlist citizen volunteers e.g. youth, neighbors, to develop companionate relationships	• develop support groups among low income female headed families to exchange day care • provide lay helpers to assist as homemakers and companions to families at risk	• develop exchange networks among citizens, families and relatives of developmentally disabled to provide respite care • use peer aids to train disabled in skills of independent living	• organize volunteers among church groups to provide companionate relationships to chronic patients • develop natural helping teams of neighbors, family and friends and service providers to assist with mentally ill	• develop resource bank to identify residents who are willing to provide services • identify and consult with group of indigenous leaders to foster community strengths • develop partnership relationships with local businesses, church and neighborhood associations to find local solutions

(Continued)

TABLE 3.1 Opportunities for Developing Linkages (continued)

		TARGET POPULATIONS		
Problem Focus	Elderly	Children, Youth and Families	Developmental and Physical Disabled	Mental Health Clients	Low Income and Ethnic Communities
Health related issues	• develop neighborhood networks of mutual aid around meal sites, meals on wheels programs	• develop mutual aid groups among mothers of infants to exchange information and support	• develop self-help among physically disabled to exchange information on self-care	• consult with board and care operators to improve identification and early intervention	• establish relationships with local grocery stores to improve availability of nutrition information
• long term care					
• nutrition			• develop parents groups in conjunction with hospitals, pediatricians to provide support to newly identified parents of developmentally disabled	• develop patient medication support groups	• identify and enlist lay facilitators to provide first aid and health information
• prevention care	• contact and consult with SRO managers to identify problems

• develop patient support groups in nursing homes | • support mutual aid groups among teenage pregnant mothers in schools | | | |

Staff of other agencies focus on the needs of a particular population group and are concerned with promoting *mutual aid* or *self-help* networks within that group. This may involve tapping into existing informal networks of mutual aid or creating self-help networks among agency clients. Whether existing or created, mutual aid networks share similarities with the helping that occurs within organized self-help groups in that individuals come together on the basis of shared problems or circumstances (Katz & Bender, 1976). The important difference is that informal mutual aid networks are generally free of the influences of formal charter and organization that characterize many organized self-help groups. Helping is more dependent on maintaining norms of reciprocity than on supporting a group identity or organized philosophy.

A third major focus is on helping networks based on *geographical propinquity*. Table 3.1 provides several examples of agencies whose program objectives were directed to community-wide issues or to populations living within a defined locality. Some of these agencies identified natural helpers who were key figures within the neighborhood; others focused on promoting neighbor-to-neighbor exchanges. While some agencies identified existing locality-based helping networks, others attempted to foster them. Staff identified various types of community representatives such as school officials, clergy, storekeepers, or simply knowledgeable residents and then organized them into helping networks.

The goals of the agencies in working with these networks generally included developing or strengthening two kinds of linkages: horizontal and vertical. Horizontal linking involves social relationships among people in similar circumstances. Agencies that help expand an individual's personal network, or bring together people with similar problems to provide mutual aid, or encourage neighbor-to-neighbor ties are creating horizontal linkages.

Vertical linking ties the individual to larger social institutions such as schools, churches, local government, or human services agencies. A major goal of most of the programs was to develop connections between the formal service system and the informal system, so that information about community services and resources would be more accessible. In addition, such linkages might serve goals of making agencies more sensitive to local needs, or developing a group's capacity to organize and advocate on its own behalf.

Both the type of network the agency chooses to work with and the linking strategy chosen are also affected by factors outside the control of the agency. The resources available to agency clientele and the different types of community members who are willing or likely to participate in the agency's program are two additional factors affecting the choice of strategy. Different strategies will imply different assignments of responsibility to informal helpers and the amount of control exercised by agency staff also will vary.

Relationships Between Staff and Helpers

Professionals and informal helpers are coming from two quite different understandings about how help is given. Professional helping is generally based on standards acquired through training and experience; knowledge and expertise are valued in establishing the credibility of the help provided. These standards may have little meaning for informal helpers, as their helping is based on informal personal relationships, shared experiences, and altruism, and their credibility is determined by the norms of exchange within the network. Both types of helping have value; the relationship formed between the two must acknowledge the value of each type while coming to terms with issues involving differences in responsibility, authority, and status.

Responsibility, authority, and status are not often explicitly decided nor are they matters which are often separable in practice. They get worked out largely as issues of control and affect such features of interaction as how helpers are recruited, the flexibility of the respective roles, the degree of staff supervision involved, and the number of different helping activities involved. For example, one indicator of the implicit choices staff make about responsibility and authority is the process of deciding how helpers will be identified and who will be involved. An approach in which staff have definite criteria for identifying helpers or require some sort of formal commitment before helpers become involved in their program indicates caution in assigning responsibility. Supervision or close monitoring of helpers' activities by staff indicates a decision to retain authority. In contrast, allowing helpers to "nominate" themselves by virtue of the activities in which they are already engaged, or encouraging helpers to determine what tasks or activities should be undertaken indicate greater willingness to share responsibility and authority.

Three different types of relationships were found to underlie the variety of linkages developed between staff and helpers in the thirty agencies. Shown in Table 3.2, these three types of relationships can be classified according to a number of characteristics which indicate how authority and responsibility are divided in carrying out the tasks or activities involved in services. The three types have been termed *coordinative, collegial,* and *directive* to suggest the quality of interaction between staff and helpers. Although the coordinative and directive relationships are at the opposite ends of the scale on a number of these characteristics, the three relationships do not fall neatly on a continuum. In practice, these relationships are affected by a variety of other factors such as those discussed earlier (e.g., the needs of the target population, the characteristics of the community). The meaning of these terms can best be understood by comparing the specific indicators which distinguish one type of relationship from another.

Coordinative. A "coordinative" type of relationship is charac-terized by a relatively high degree of independent action in which helpers decide what they will work on, take more responsibility for tasks and activities, and receive little or no supervision from agency staff. Individual staff can substitute for each other in their work with different helpers so that relationships are less exclusive. Staff and helpers work on many different tasks together and the role played by helpers changes over time. This type of relationship is illustrated by one program in which staff have organized task forces of neighbors to provide services to elderly persons living in an inner city neighbor-hood. Helpers form neighborhood teams and take most of the respon-sibility for providing help. Agency staff coordinate the separate activities of the neighborhood teams in order to assure an integrated range of services from home maintenance to social and health services.

Collegial. In comparison to the coordinative relationship, a "collegial" relationship is characterized less by independence and more by interdependence. Staff do not supervise or monitor helpers, although they are more systematic in the way they identify and recruit participants. The relationship is more particularized between an individual staff member and an individual helper. Helpers do not have to make a formal commitment to become involved. Staff and

TABLE 3.2 Relationships Between Staff and Helpers

Classification Items*	Coordinative	Collegial	Directive
Staff identify and recruit helpers through systematic procedures	L	M	H
Staff just seem to involve helpers in course of their work	M	H	L
Helpers must make formal commitment to become involved	M	L	H
Individual helper's role may change over time	H	M	L
Staff and helpers work on many different tasks and activities	H	L	L
Helpers take responsibility for tasks and activities	H	M	L
Individual staff and helpers have exclusive, one-to-one relationships	L	H	M
Staff supervise helpers	L	L	H
Helpers work on staff-determined tasks	M	L	H
Staff substitute for each other in working with different helpers	H	M	L
Staff monitor helpers' work	L	L	H
Helpers seek out staff for help	H	L	L

*   Discriminant function of cluster analysis:
      canonical correlation = .92; $p < .001$
      prediction results = 90% cases correctly classified; $p < .001$.
** Key: H = above mean score for all groups
         M = about equal to mean score
         L = below mean score

helpers share the responsibility of deciding what is to be done. Because of interdependence and shared authority in the context of more exclusive, one-to-one relationships, these relationships are similar to those between two colleagues. An agency working with an elderly clientele provides an illustration of a collegial relationship. In the course of providing services, staff, with the permission of the client, work to identify and encourage the participation of family members, relatives, friends, and neighbors known to an elderly client. Periodically, staff contact these helpers by phone, consult them about problems of the client, provide encouragement for what the individual has been doing, and ask if any assistance is needed.

Directive. In contrast to the collegial and coordinative relationships a "directive" relationship is more restrictive in the degree of responsibility and authority accorded informal helpers. Staff systematically recruit helpers, often requiring a formal commitment from those selected. The helpers' activities are supervised and monitored. They work on more limited, staff-determined tasks, and their roles are less likely to change over time. An agency concerned with promoting independent living for the severely disabled illustrates the more directive relationship. Staff identify individuals who are particularly knowledgeable or skillful in respect to some aspect of independent living, such as making use of public transportation or supervising attendant care. Such individuals are asked to provide training to severely disabled clients on the subject of their expertise. Agency staff decide on what subjects helpers will provide instruction as well as the manner in which training will be provided. In these respects, staff play a more directive role in the way responsibility is assigned to helpers.

These three types of relationships—coordinative, collegial, directive—illustrate how the questions of who has what responsibility and authority in carrying out the tasks of service delivery can be decided. We have focused on control issues because they are a very important aspect of the relationship. The examples presented above demonstrate, however, that each of these relationships allows a more autonomous role for the informal helpers than is generally found in human service programs that incorporate volunteers.

A Typology of Agency Strategies

We compared the three alternative relationships developed between staff and helpers with the types of helping networks involved to examine the program strategies agencies adopted (Froland et al., 1979). Shown in Table 3.3, five types of strategies were identified. The first, *personal networks,* focused on an individual client's support system. Agency staff provided consultation and assistance to sustain and reinforce the informal efforts of family, friends, and neighbors known to a client. Another strategy, *volunteer linking,* was adopted in situations where existing sources of personal support were limited and involved matching lay helpers to clients to provide companionship, support, and advocacy. A third strategy, *mutual aid networks,* was the most common approach utilized by the agencies in the sample and involved the development of links between individuals who shared common problems, interests, or backgrounds for the purpose of sharing resources and reducing social isolation. The last two strategies were directed to a neighborhood or community. The *neighborhood helper* strategy involved identifying central figures in a neighborhood who are performing key helping roles informally and developing a consultative relationship to support existing patterns of help and to prevent the need for formal services. The fifth strategy, *community empowerment,* involved the development of ties among informal opinion leaders within a community to plan improvements in services and to identify existing resources for meeting needs. As we discuss in Chapter 5, these five strategies were most often combined in a coordinated program for working with informal sources of help. In the following sections each strategy is described in more detail, giving attention to the general focus and aims, the interaction between staff and helpers, and the implications of adopting the strategy. Case examples of each strategy are also provided.

PERSONAL NETWORKS STRATEGY

This approach focuses on the existing relationships of a client or on the potential relationships that may be developed within the client's natural setting. The client's personal network usually includes family, friends, and neighbors. Key members of a client's personal network may be identified as helpers by the client or staff may reach out to encourage relationships with those friends or relations of a client who are willing and able to help. A number of agencies have adopted the strategy of listing all existing and potential relationships a client may have available as part of the intake interview and creating a file for keeping track of an individual's network in the course of services. Staff efforts are directed to strengthening the existing relationships in the network, renewing old relationships or establishing new ones. In our study, most of the agencies that adopted this strategy were concerned with elderly clients, although some programs had adopted it in work with families or the mentally ill.

In most of the agencies that adopted the personal networks strategy, more than three staff persons (sometimes peer counselors) were involved, each of whom spent more than 50 percent of their

TABLE 3.3 A Typology of Program Strategies

Strategies	Objectives	Informal Helping Networks	Relationship
Personal network	consult with client's significant others; supporting existing efforts	family members, friends, neighbors, service providers	primarily collegial
	convene network of providers and family, friends and others to resolve problems		
	expand client's range of social ties		
Volunteer linking	provide lay therapists for counseling	citizen volunteers	primarily directive
	establish companionate relationships	people with skills, interests relevant to client's needs	
	recruit and link volunteer advocates to client	people with similar experience	
Mutual aid networks	establish peer support groups	local church associates	more collegial with existing network
	consult with existing groups and support activities	clients with similar problems	
		people with shared concerns	either directive or coordinative for created networks
Neighborhood helpers	establish consultative arrangement with neighbor to monitor problems	neighbors	more collegial but may be coordinative
		clerks, managers in local businesses	
	convene neighbors to promote local helping	religious leaders	
Community empowerment	establish local task forces for meeting community needs	opinion leaders in local business, religious institutions	primarily coordinative
	provide for community forums to have input into local policies	members of local voluntary associations	
		neighborhood leaders	

work time on this effort. Staff usually worked with fewer than five informal helpers for each client. The clients tended to have small helping networks, usually of less than ten members. Relationships between staff and helpers were largely informal and collegial, with staff interacting with informal helpers within a client's network on a one-to-one basis through phone calls or visits. The general aim was to encourage members of the network to continue to support the client. Often the contact with the agency had been initiated by the client or the helper because a crisis had developed, and the staff role was to help resolve the crisis. Contact with staff was more frequent initially, usually on a weekly basis, tapering off over the course of several months to monthly contacts. While the expected duration of the relationship between the informal helpers and the client was open-ended, most program staff generally ended contact with informal helpers after two to three months. However, in situations where staff worked with clients over a longer period, the relationship with helpers also tended to be more long term.

An agency dealing with an elderly population provides an example of the kinds of purposes this approach may serve:

> *The purpose of* the individual services component of the agency is to work with the informal supports of the older person as well as with the older person to make decisions about formal service needs. The emphasis of the program is on supporting the *caregivers* of the elderly, so that they are able to continue in their role, keeping the older person out of an institution for as long as that is possible or reasonable. The program allows the caregivers rather than staff to make decisions about the services needed. Staff provide counseling, housekeeping, homecare, and other services when appropriate.
>
> [*Case No. 4*]

Another agency offers a picture of how the personal network strategy can be implemented and also illustrates the collegial nature of the relationship that develops:

> *Most clients are* referred by other agencies and are asked at intake who has helped them before, what help has been provided, and who the client's family, friends, and relations are. A file sheet records potential contacts which individual staff followup on to establish a relationship. Staff often first visit the "referrals"—sometimes neighbors, sometimes family members—to make contact, to let them know the agency

is working with the client, and to set an expectation of cooperation in helping the elderly client. From time to time, usually every one to three months unless a crisis emerges, staff will phone the significant others to "check in," monitor their relationship with the client, and discuss what problems might be occurring.

The relationship is informal, neighborly, but limited to an individual staff member, a client, and their significant others. This means that although staff may exchange information among themselves, only a crisis will provide cause for a field counselor who has not had contact with an elderly client's support system to contact a member of that system. This may not be so much a matter of confidentiality as it is a reflection of who knows whom, and who has established a basis for communication. In all, the process appears to be distinguished by informality and cooperation.

[*Case No. 7*]

The primary contribution of this strategy lies in its emphasis on the client's significant others for problem-solving, social reintegration, and social responsibility for the client's progress. By becoming directly involved in efforts to reinforce the supportive capacities of an individual's personal network, program staff are able to both enhance an individual's chances for successful resolution of the immediate problem and to promote independence and coping abilities over the long run. Additionally, by using informal helpers in the client's network, staff resources can be extended to a larger number of clients.

There are a number of difficulties involved with implementing the personal network strategy. First, the strategy must deal with the question of confidentiality because of the client's need for privacy in respect to significant others. The problem of resolving conflicts within the network, dealing with parts of the network which foster client behaviors with problematic consequences, or working with clients who are extremely socially isolated constitute additional issues for staff. Finally, for clients with severe problems or limitations, either short- or long-term in nature, the ability of the personal network to provide a sustained supportive response may be limited. As a result, most programs utilizing this strategy integrated it with an array of formal services as well as other strategies such as linking clients to mutual aid networks or neighborhood helpers.

VOLUNTEER LINKING STRATEGY

The purpose of the volunteer linking strategy is to develop one-to-one relationships between people undergoing crisis or needing support and advocacy for long-term adjustment and informal helpers who can successfully provide advice, support, and personal commitment. Staff efforts are focused on matching clients with individuals who have been recruited for their personal experience with problems a client may have or simply for their willingness to provide help. Staff use a variety of ways to identify prospective helpers. Some approaches such as advertising are similar to those employed to recruit more traditional volunteers. More often, staff rely on more informal recruitment techniques. For example, one program serving the physically disabled uses informal contacts and word of mouth referrals to identify individuals who could be of help to disabled clients preparing to reenter the community. Some programs use other clients who have made successful adjustments as helpers. Often, helpers are self-referred. Because of the degree to which the agency feels responsible for what the helpers do in this approach, program staff usually screen helpers and confer with clients in order to facilitate successful matches. Most of the agencies in our study that were utilizing this strategy were serving the developmentally or physically disabled and were working to promote the client's successful functioning in the community. Other agencies had adopted the strategy in their work with elderly clients, with families undergoing crisis situations, or with the chronically mentally ill.

In each agency, only a few paid staff were assigned to the task of recruiting and matching volunteers, usually less than five but most often only one or two. These staff usually spent less than 50 percent of their work effort on the volunteer linking strategy. The number of helpers that staff were working with was usually less than ten, although in several agencies more than twenty helpers were involved. Indeed, one agency that was concerned with developing "citizen advocates" for developmentally disabled individuals had developed over one hundred successful matches. Most often, the size of the helping network that was enlisted by the helper on behalf of a client was small, involving less than ten people. Staff and helpers usually met together on a one-to-one basis, sometimes in combination with group meetings. Generally, staff adopted a directive relationship with helpers which involved training and supervision. However, in one instance where parents of developmentally disabled children were recruited to provide support to parents of newly identified developmentally disabled children, staff relationships with helpers were very informal and involved no training. Contact between client and helpers usually occurred on at least a weekly basis, although the expected duration of the relationship varied with a client's problems. Crisis situations, or short-term needs for support, involved relationships of roughly two to three months, while long-term adjustment involved more open-ended relationships. Staff usually were in contact with helpers on a monthly basis, with the duration of their relationships with helpers being relatively open-ended.

A program serving the physically disabled illustrates some of the ways volunteer helpers can be identified and recruited to contribute specific skills:

> *A central part of* promoting community integration of clients involves the use of nonprofessional resource persons in the community. These individuals, usually disabled, are selectively recruited and paid to provide training to agency clients in a skill needed for living independently in the community. The job of identification and recruitment falls on the staff associate coordinator, a disabled individual with a wide range of contacts within the handicapped community. The coordinator goes about identifying individuals in several ways; for instance, a roster is kept of people who have served in the past, who are contacted to see whether they are interested in doing a training module or if they know of someone else; sometimes the "grapevine" is set in motion by numerous phone calls; announcements are advertised; sometimes the coordinator knows of someone through her network.

> Individuals are recruited because they have special knowledge or skills in one of the training areas of independent living. For example, one individual was recruited for the module on living arrangements because he had experienced the gamut of possible living situations. He had lived with family members and in nursing homes and apartment clusters, and had ultimately set up his own cooperative living arrangement. As a result, he had acquired unique insights into the problems and possibilities associated with each type of arrangement. Another individual was recruited for a session on performance of physical tasks. She was a quadraplegic with severe limitations in physical mobility but had successfully managed a law practice by learning how to run several office machines specially modified for her abilities.

Not only do staff associates have concrete skills they are able to teach disabled clients, but they also serve as role models demonstrating a lifestyle and an approach to living independently. They also serve as informal contact brokers for clients, suggesting individuals or agencies in the community that may be helpful.

[*Case No. 15*]

In this example, the role of the volunteer helper is to teach special skills or knowledge, although opportunity for social and recreational contact does occur. Another example from an agency dealing with child abuse and neglect illustrates a role in which companionship and social support is provided by a volunteer helper:

The "*lay therapist*" approach is a home-based intervention for clients identified as having problems with child abuse. The therapist comes to the home as a "friend" and focuses on positive interactions. Therapists are often accepted by the clients more readily than a professional because they have time to build a relationship based on trust. The client soon learns that the therapist helps in concrete ways and does not force the client to make decisions or take initiatives for which they are not ready. The therapists do not represent authority; they are rarely used to present testimony regarding a client in court, and they can assure the clients that their involvement with them is totally voluntary.

[*Case No. 12*]

There are several strengths to the volunteer linking strategy. First, a client's need for intimate support can be more efficiently filled by a person who has similar background or experience and who may often serve as a role model. Staff can help many more clients through the use of lay helpers than if they were involved in providing sustained support themselves. Helpers may also link clients to members of their own network, contributing to the adjustment of disabled clients.

The major difficulty of the approach involves creating successful matches, particularly when the aim is to develop sustained relationships. However, programs with several years' experience appear to have developed expertise in promoting compatible relationships and in orienting helpers to clients. A number of agencies have adopted the strategy as an independent service but the experience of other agencies in our study suggests the strategy is enhanced by the availability of support services and of other informal helping strategies, e.g., mutual aid networks.

MUTUAL AID NETWORKS

The mutual aid networks strategy focuses on actual or potential relationships among a set of individuals who come together because they have experienced similar problems, face common tasks, or have compatible interests or abilities. While mutual aid networks are similar in purpose to self-help organizations, they are less formally organized, usually without an official charter, explicit ideology, or standardized program. In adopting a mutual aid strategy, staff may aim their efforts in a number of directions. First, they may attempt to establish ties to existing mutual aid groups in an effort to provide consultation and support to sustain existing efforts. Staff may also work to create mutual aid networks among present and former clients who share problems and among clients and informal helpers in the community as a way to develop sources of support for continuing needs. Finally, staff may also organize mutual aid networks for advocacy purposes as a way of creating a forum for a population of individuals at risk.

In this respect, mutual aid networks can be classified according to two different types of orientations: Type I and Type II (Tracy & Gassow, 1976). Type I refers to an inner orientation in which members are concerned, share problems and feelings, and provide support and assistance to other members. In contrast, Type II networks are externally oriented and members direct their energies to broader issues and rights, often advocating their concerns by lobbying or legislative activities.

More than two-thirds of the agencies we studied had adopted a mutual aid network strategy. Most of the time, staff were working with a Type I network. In a number of instances, however, the network incorporated both a Type I and Type II orientation. In only one instance was the network exclusively Type II. Agencies employing the mutual aid strategy were working with a diverse set of problems including the elderly and their caregivers, widows, new mothers, the developmentally disabled and their parents, those with mental health problems such as the chronically mentally ill, and even such specific problems as agoraphobia. Staff in many agencies had organized more than one group.

The number of paid staff devoting time to this strategy varied widely among the agencies. Most agencies used less than five paid staff, who in turn spent less than 50 percent of their overall effort in this area. Staff usually only worked with those group members who had leadership roles or were key helpers, although everyone in mutual aid networks is considered a helper. While the number of key helpers within one given mutual aid network varied, staff were typically in contact with about twenty helpers. The size of the mutual aid networks tended to be less than thirty members, with many having less than ten members. However, in several instances, staff had developed networks of nearly a hundred individuals. Contact between staff and key helpers most often occurred in group situations, although more informal contacts also occurred on a one-to-one basis. Most often, staff developed informal collegial relationships with helpers, although sometimes training, orientation, or supervision were emphasized. Helpers were in contact with other members of the network on a weekly or at least monthly basis; staff contact with helpers usually took place with similar frequency. The expected duration of the relationships among the network's helpers and staff was generally open-ended.

The work of an elderly services program within a large community mental health center illustrates how complex existing networks of mutual aid within a community may be and the kind of role played by agency staff:

> *Three major mutual aid* networks had been identified in areas with a high proportion of senior citizens. Two emerged within different low income housing complexes that accommodated the elderly. One was started in 1971 in the first housing complex to be constructed, Fellowship House I, and had grown to include roughly 75 active members. The members of the network had elected a core group of leaders but met monthly to plan and organize recreational outings, arts and crafts projects, and educational programs. Space for meetings was provided by the administrator of the complex, a pastor. To manage expenses, the club charged members $2.00 per year in dues.

> With the opening of Fellowship House II, many members of the network transferred residence and soon organized a new club along similar lines. This new seniors' club became more active because of the age and energy of new members. Together, the two seniors' clubs at the two Fellowship House complexes have provided a broad range of social activities for members as well as helping to orient and integrate new residents.

The third informal mutual aid network identified was called Friendship Club of Hunter's Woods and had a membership of nearly eighty seniors, fifty years old or older. The Club began in 1974, and had a predominantly single female membership with few single males or married couples. This Club was perhaps the most active of the three and in fact drew members from other organizations including the Fellowship House II Seniors' Club. Most members were more financially secure than the other two clubs and many lived independently in condominiums or nonsubsidized apartments.

While the focus of the three clubs was centered around social and recreational outings, the groups also provided a major vehicle for displaced elderly to meet new people and get involved in friendship circles. In addition, a major consequence of the clubs was an informal network of mutual aid whereby members would contact each other outside of organized group activities.

The posture of the staff was first to understand the strengths of this network and second to develop a working relationship with key figures within the network. The staff were concerned to play a complementary role and were sensitive to the need to affirm the self-determination of individual self-help groups. For example, one of the issues that surfaced in several clubs was how to encourage more activity among members so they would not rely on one or two leaders within each group. The task for staff was to provide organizational consultation designed to strengthen the cohesiveness of the self-help group membership. At the same time, the staff role was to be an advisor to such groups and to help out when asked, but not to play an active part in the ongoing business of each club. In this way, open lines of communication were maintained without staff "taking over" the self-help efforts of the network.

[Case No. 6]

Another agency working with a more severely impaired population of chronically mentally ill patients illustrates how mutual aid networks can be developed when existing sources of support are lacking:

The focus of staff effort centers on a network of mutual aid and self-help among nearly one hundred ex-mental patients. The overall network has been subdivided into four local networks based on geographical clustering of members so as to increase the accessibility of members to regularly scheduled network activities. Subnetworks range in size from about ten to forty active members.

Staff work with members on several different types of activities to promote social interaction and develop supportive relationships. Regularly scheduled area meetings provide an opportunity for members within a particular area to get to know each other on an informal basis to plan and to participate in social and recreational activities. Periodic general network meetings, a newsletter, and a membership directory provide vehicles for keeping in touch with the whole network. Member-organized fundraising activities such as car washes, dances, and bake sales provide ways to finance more expensive outings and events. Staff also provide educational activities through skill training materials and programs. Community Living Skill Training modules are made available to members and include such topics as job hunting, problem-solving, and others. Other services include crisis support, advocacy, information on and referral to community resources. Staff have also assisted members to develop and run a cooperative living facility in cooperation with a halfway house.

[*Case No. 21*]

The mutual aid network strategy has a number of positive values, as reflected in the number of agencies who have utilized it. First, mutual aid networks promote normalization and social integration among clients as well as a sense of confidence and self-esteem in sharing problems and helping others. Members can find and provide support without feelings of stigma or dependency. Members are encouraged to take responsibility for their problems and mutual aid networks have the potential for serving as a base for advocating for individual rights. Finally, for staff, the strategy offers a great deal of flexibility and is suitable for a wide range of problems. By emphasizing members as helpers, the strategy can also help to maximize the use of staff resources.

There are also a number of difficulties associated with this strategy. Often, encouraging and sustaining mutual aid requires self-initiation and motivation among members. This may be a difficult task for people with problems which are socially limiting in nature, e.g., the isolated elderly, the developmentally or mentally disabled. A major issue for staff of many agencies has been how to balance needs for outside assistance with the need to mobilize members to continue unaided. Mutual aid efforts are often immobilized by crisis situations, conflicts among members, or leadership cliques, or simply are of uneven value for all members. Many agencies have recognized a need for backup services to sustain member involvement. In more active networks, some agencies have recognized the possibility of expanding the network to include neighborhood helpers.

NEIGHBORHOOD HELPING NETWORKS

The neighborhood helping network strategy directs an agency's efforts toward identifying informal helping networks in the context of a geographically defined community. Sometimes, emphasis is given to finding existing natural helpers in a neighborhood area who play instrumental roles in providing a wide range of assistance to others. The process of identifying and forming relationships with neighborhood helpers is multifaceted and complex. Most often, staff begin by spending a great deal of time canvassing the community, talking to residents, and learning about the informal norms and social organization of specific neighborhoods. Neighborhood helpers come to be identified by "reputation" when several residents mention the helpful role an individual has been performing. Referrals also may come from community-based organizations or voluntary associations, from a clergy member or other informal leader, or sometimes from clients who consistently mention a particular person as being helpful. Those helpers who have been identified are often useful in identifying other potential helpers. The process of recruiting helpers is usually fairly informal, often just contacting and chatting with the individual about the neighborhood. "Recruitment" may simply mean forming a friendship and may not involve explicit invitations or requests to participate in agency-sponsored activities. This strategy may also include a variety of other ways of working with the neighborhood and other kinds of helpers, i.e., neighbors and role-related helpers. Staff work in collaboration with neighborhood helpers to help isolated individuals, promote mutual aid among neighborhood residents, identify emerging local issues, and strengthen informal social organization within the neighborhood. Many of the agencies that have adopted this strategy are working with targeted problems such as the elderly, the developmentally disabled, and the chronically mentally ill, although the majority of agencies are concerned with more preventive aims directed to a general community population.

Within most agencies, a relatively small number of staff were assigned to work on this strategy, usually less than five and often only one or two. In a few instances, however, five to ten staff members were involved. Most often, those who were working on this strategy spent more than 50 percent of their time in this way. Staff were generally involved with a large number of informal helpers, usually more than ten helpers and sometimes in excess of twenty helpers. The size of the helpers' networks varied considerably. At a minimum, most staff were working with helpers who were part of networks of between ten and thirty members. Very often, staff interacted with neighborhood helpers on a one-to-one basis. In those instances where group meetings were employed, staff also incorporated individual contact. In general, staff relationships with helpers were primarily informal and collegial, characterized by mutual respect and equal status in helping roles. The amount and expected duration of contact between staff and helpers and helpers and networks was fairly uniform. Staff had at least monthly contact with helpers, and often weekly contact, and the relationships were expected to continue indefinitely. Helpers saw others in the neighborhood network frequently, usually every week, and relationships within the network were ongoing.

One senior center serving elderly residents of a neighborhood illustrates how the use of block workers may facilitate neighborhood helping networks:

> *Through their outreach* work in the neighborhood and their contacts with block workers and with the elderly who use the center, the staff have discovered people who provide some kind of assistance on a regular or irregular basis to one of the elderly residents of the neighborhood. They use this growing fund of knowledge about the helping system to find informal help for other elderly residents. They may encourage such helping by simply letting it be known that someone has a problem—perhaps a need for the lawn to be mowed or small services during an illness; a simple mention is usually enough to spark spontaneous offers to help or visit. In other cases, the staff may be able to suggest what an older person could offer in return for help, for many are reluctant to accept help if they cannot reciprocate. Their work with both block workers and the neighborhood helping system is aimed at making the resources of the center a part of the neighborhood and at making the helping system work better.
>
> [*Case No. 2*]

The neighborhood helping strategy can also be directed to integrating a socially isolated population into a community. This is illustrated by an agency whose staff provides follow-up support to mentally and developmentally disabled clients:

> *Two staff members provide* opportunities for the clients to take part in activities in the surrounding community and to develop their social networks. The staff try in a variety of ways to make connections between the clients and informal helping resources in the community. This may involve developing situations where clients mingle with community people. For example, one of the staff and some of the clients have begun to volunteer to cook dinner one night a week at a local cafe run entirely by volunteers, where clients and cafe "regulars" from the community mingle at dinner. In addition to helping clients feel comfortable in existing community settings, they create new situations where clients and community can meet, such as sponsoring a dance with music by a local women's band or organizing a softball team that plays other teams in the community. They also encourage the clients to develop relationships with other clients, and to take part individually or in small groups in ongoing activities in the community.
> [*Case No. 19*]

A final example of the neighborhood helping strategy illustrates how staff roles can serve more preventive aims:

> *The goal is to* understand the natural helping system and the community resources: natural helpers, special skills, and local concerns. The staff role is to become an added resource to help the local residents accomplish what *they* feel is important. Where the standard social service agency "does things for" people, staff feel it is important to ask "What do *you* want to do, and how can we help you?"

> Two staff members are referred to as natural helper facilitators. They are responsible for identifying and working with natural helpers, particularly those who provide direct personal assistance to their own circle of neighbors and friends—as advisors, "good neighbors," "play ladies," and so on. The natural helper facilitators follow the "good neighbor" strategy—they stop by to visit, call occasionally, listen, share information, act as consultants. They are also responsible for finding out how the natural helpers' efforts can be enhanced by the addition of tangible resources.

> There is one staff member, a network developer, who is responsible for increasing the size of the local resource base by encouraging linkages between natural helpers with common service concerns—recreation

for kids, crime prevention, neighborhood maintenance, and jobs. This
is a coordinating/mobilizing/facilitation role that requires sensitivity
to what works and what will best meet what the community wants.

[*Case No. 25*]

This strategy recognizes that neighborhood helpers are effective in
strengthening mutual aid among residents, in helping to integrate
individuals into the community, and in providing windows to the
informal strengths of the neighborhood. Staff may effectively reach
an entire community through a manageable number of individuals
who are central linking and referral agents within the informal social
organization of a community. These connections with a community
extend professional resources and identify instances where formal
intervention is appropriate. The promise of the strategy depends both
on being able to find key helping figures and on developing appropriate
relationships between staff and helpers.

Several difficulties have been encountered by staff in agencies
adopting this strategy. Entering the informal world of a neighborhood, identifying strengths among unknown residents, and developing
a sensitivity to local norms and culture is a task requiring staff
flexibility and openness and also the availability of personal support
for this new role. Setting appropriate expectations, locating key
people in deteriorated or transient neighborhoods, and finding the
best way to use professional expertise are some of the major issues
that confront staff. Staff turnover, agency efforts that are limited by
time constraints, and needs for formalized activities are also factors
which may undermine the feasibility of this strategy. Although the
strategy may be implemented in a surprisingly diverse range of
neighborhoods from inner city to rural areas, many agencies incorporate other services when working with severe problems. It is often
employed in conjunction with other ways of promoting informal
helping such as personal network or mutual aid strategies.

COMMUNITY EMPOWERMENT NETWORKS

This last strategy is somewhat similar to the neighborhood helper
strategy in that the focus is on identifying and working with key
figures in a geographically defined community. The difference
reflects a political emphasis, for key figures in this approach are more
often opinion leaders and key representatives of an area than those
individuals who have informal ties to a helping network. There are
times, however, when the same people are involved in both kinds of

activities. Staff efforts in developing community empowerment networks are directed to identifying and establishing a forum for informal leaders within a community who can effectively represent a range of informal interest groups. Staff identify informal leaders in a manner similar to the neighborhood helper strategy (e.g., canvassing) except that the focus is usually shifted to find those who are particularly helpful in advocating for others or those to whom other people turn when something needs to be done or a decision needs to be made. Informal leaders often emerge from neighborhood-based voluntary associations, local businesses, professional groups, and religious institutions. Once identified, informal leaders are usually asked to become involved in group activities centered around community wide problem-solving. The leaders become a voice for the community, articulating local problems but also developing a recognition of the community's own strengths and informal resources.

The strategy can sometimes be implemented by only one or two professionals. Some agencies employed from three to five staff members who functioned as a team. Staff were most often employed full-time on this strategy and were in contact with between five to twenty key figures, each of whom was in contact with between twenty and thirty other individuals in the community on a regular basis. Staff and leaders generally met as a group on a weekly basis. The relationship between staff and community representatives could be characterized as coordinative in that staff facilitated meetings and assisted in working out issues, but did not act in a supervisory capacity. The expected duration of the relationship was long-term and open to continuing developments.

An agency working with a small rural community which has a population of about 7000 residents provides an example of how the strategy may be implemented:

> *The major thrust* of the project so far has been to work with the community, with the belief that until the community's existing resources are mobilized, individual client needs cannot be effectively addressed by the community. Additionally, the project seeks to develop an ongoing capacity that will remain when funds for the project run out. Activities have been carried out such as canvassing neighborhoods; talking with citizens, the business community, religious institutions and civic organizations, local government; meeting

with other formal service providers; and organizing special interest committees to articulate and discuss community needs. These efforts have developed support for the project within the community and helped to identify and enlist its natural resources to meet the needs of its residents.

[*Case No. 27*]

The strategy can also be applied to urban communities. One agency in the study working to improve the appropriateness of mental health services to inner city neighborhoods with strong ethnic traditions (in this case a Polish Catholic working class neighborhood) provides an illustration:

Working through an organization representing the varied sectors of the neighborhood, staff identified the strengths and resources used by area residents to solve mental health problems, and some of the needs that residents felt were still unmet by the local helping network and the professional service system. Pilot projects were developed to meet these needs. The pilot projects involved committees of volunteers from the community planning programs in consultation with professionals from local agencies. Each pilot project committee was structured in a manner which put community residents in control of activities and agendas. The first pilot project involved the preparation of a Referral Directory listing helping agencies and groups serving the neighborhood. A second major problem area identified was family communications, for which a series of workshops and skits were developed. Subsequently, staff worked with a wide range of pilot project committees: Family Communications, Widowed Persons with Dependent Children, Widowed Persons, Youth Committee, Clergy/Agency Committee, Wellness Project, Senior Citizens, Separated/Divorced, and Agoraphobic Groups.

[*Case No. 28*]

The major contribution offered by the community empowerment strategy lies in its potential for mobilizing an effective body of representatives who can articulate both the need for formal services as well as the ways in which they may be appropriately integrated with the community's own resources. In this way, the community comes to feel ownership of programs and services as well as responsibility for problems and issues that need to be worked out. The strategy also can be an effective vehicle for working on problems relating to a specific client population.

The major difficulties associated with this strategy stem from potential political conflicts that may emerge. Factions or competing interest groups may develop to advocate for different priorities and some constituencies may not be represented if they are poorly organized. The neutrality of staff is central to their role as facilitators, but this may be hard to maintain in the face of conflicting demands. If staff align themselves with a particular interest, they may effectively close off options with other groups. Furthermore, the scope of issues arising from a community-wide attempt at problem-solving is often broader than the specific goals of the organization within which staff are working. Needs may be identified that staff are unequipped to handle, thereby creating frustration among community members. To the extent that community members can be encouraged to take responsibility for the process, however, many of these difficulties can be worked out satisfactorily.

Conclusion

This chapter has discussed how staff in the agencies we have studied have developed ways to ally themselves with informal helping networks in order to provide different kinds of human services. Philosophies, ideologies, relationships and strategies have been described to suggest how professional providers and informal caregivers can engage in a mutually beneficial partnership. Because of the nature of our study, the views we have presented for working with informal helpers are seen through the eyes of professional helpers operating within a formal human service system. From a broader perspective, this may tell us more about how professionals see themselves relating formal services to informal sources of care than about how informal helpers see the relationship between the help they provide and formal human service organizations. Were we to adopt the perspective of informal caregivers, perhaps a different picture would emerge to suggest how professionals and informal sources of care could work together.

Nevertheless, the strategies described show that within the present constitution of human service organizations it is both possible and practical to begin developing a partnership between professional and informal helping resources. These strategies offer a preliminary set of tools that can be refined and extended to new situations as other agencies and professionals resolve to become more aware of and sensitive to the myriad ways that people help each other in daily life.

Chapter 4

CONSIDERING COSTS AND CONSEQUENCES

In previous chapters we have described some of the major features of informal helping networks and presented several strategies whereby professionals can enlist, support, or develop this resource in the course of providing agency services. These chapters address the what and how of working with informal helping. We must also consider the benefits and costs of developing a partnership between professionals and informal helpers. Can the amount of time and effort staff devote to working with informal caregivers be justified by improvements in services to clients or to the community? What sorts of expenditures of staff resources are required for different problems and what kinds of outcomes can be expected from adopting different strategies?

In this chapter, we will draw upon evidence from the thirty agencies in our study to clarify the costs and consequences of their efforts to develop professional partnerships with informal sources of help. In particular we will identify the major program costs involved in working with informal helpers, see how these costs differ depending on the nature of the problems being addressed or the alternative strategies employed, and outline the consequences of different collaborative strategies.

Cost Factors

The costs of developing and implementing one or more of the five alternative strategies discussed earlier can be examined at two levels of analysis: costs borne by an agency and external costs. Agency costs are those resource allocations made by the agency in areas such as staff time, payment to helpers, use of facilities, and overhead costs. External costs are a more indirect and often intangible aspect of social resource allocations involving shifts in the burden of costs as a consequence of utilizing informal helpers. Such shifts may occur in the demand for services (e.g., reducing or increasing demand), who provides services (e.g., referrals to other service agencies in the community) or the value of tasks performed by helpers once performed by staff (e.g., greater reliance on family members for assistance). External costs are important for understanding the true impact on public/private resource allocation for care, but are also more difficult to measure and apportion (Davies, 1980). Our focus in this chapter is on understanding agency program costs, recognizing that this area represents only part of the resource question associated with linking formal and informal care but one which is particularly crucial to program decisions.

Because the thirty agencies varied considerably in the types of staff employed; the size, location, and nature of program facilities utilized; their administrative structures; and the degree of program involvement with helpers, we do not examine program costs from a strictly quantitative, accounting viewpoint. Rather, our consideration of costs seeks to identify those common elements of procedure and staff utilization that have implications for program resource requirements. We consider six major factors that have implications for program investment in working with helpers. These are:

- *Staff effort:* number of full time equivalent (FTE) staff assigned to working with helpers; average percentage of time each staff member devotes to working with helpers; the amount of time staff spend with helpers on an informal, unstructured basis;

- *Staff coordination:* the extent to which the program has established formal mechanisms (e.g., meetings, written procedures) for coordination among staff who work with helpers;

- *Recruitment and training:* the extent to which formal procedures have been established for the identification and recruitment of helpers; the extent to which a formal program of training is provided to helpers upon recruitment into the program;

- *Supervision of helpers:* the extent to which staff review, monitor, and supervise helper activities; the extent to which staff assume overall responsibility for the tasks that helpers perform; the extent to which staff coordinate different tasks among different helpers;

- *Payment:* the extent to which helpers are provided a stipend or reimbursed for out-of-pocket expenses;

- *Backup services:* the extent to which a particular approach to working with helpers requires the availability or use of supplementary professional or agency services.

Program strategies were rated as to the degree to which they incorporated the six cost factors (see Table 4.1). On the whole, investment of agency resources was quite limited. Roughly two-thirds of the agencies assigned fewer than five staff FTE to working with helpers; one-third operated with less than three staff FTE. A little more than half of the agencies assigned staff full time to work with helpers. Most often the costs involved in recruitment, training, and supervision of helpers were minimal, as only about one-third of the agencies incurred these costs "often" or "always." Most agencies sought to coordinate the efforts of staff working with helpers, and established mechanisms for peer review, staff consultation, and communication. Almost two-thirds of the agencies in the study offered no payment at all. Overall, the major resource investments involved in working with helpers were concentrated on the amount and use of staff time and on providing for the availability of backup services.

PROBLEM TYPE AND COST

Only a very general assessment of costs can be drawn by looking at the relative degree to which the thirty agencies used various resources in implementing programs. Clearly the cost of working with helpers will depend upon the types of problems of concern to the program. Different problems place different demands on staff time and activities, and require a different level of skill, experience, or effort of helpers. More difficult problems may require greater investment in time and effort.

The thirty agencies were directed to a variety of target populations but within these populations, five major types of problems were being addressed by the alternative program strategies:

- needs for material assistance such as help with gaining employment, finding housing, or obtaining food;

TABLE 4.1 Frequency of Cost Factors

Cost Factor		Frequency Distribution (number of agencies, N = 30)			
		Never	*Some-times*	*Often*	*Always*
Supervisory					
• staff supervise or monitor helpers		7	16	4	3
• staff assume responsibility for helper activities		9	15	5	1
• staff coordinate helper activities		9	16	1	4
Recruitment and Training					
• use of formal procedures for recruitment of helpers		7	16	4	3
• use of explicit training program for helpers		11	11	3	5
Staff Coordination					
• use of mechanism for staff coordination		0	3	9	18
Payment					
• helpers are paid (stipend or reimbursement)		18	10	2	0
Backup Services					
• helper activities use available backup agency services		2	10	14	4
Staff effort					
• staff often spend time on informal canvassing or contact with helpers		6	17	4	3
• Staff FTE assigned:	less than 3 FTE	10			
	3 to 5 FTE	9			
	5 to 7 FTE	7			
	more than 7 FTE	4			
• % time of average staff member:	less than 25%	2			
	25 to 50%	2			
	50 to 75%	4			
	75 to 100%	5			
	Full time	17			

- problems related to infringements of personal rights needing individual advocacy;
- difficulties associated with community adjustment, social functioning, or activities of daily living;
- multiple problems of living, chronic conditions, and family burden;
- neighborhood problems, community development.

Program strategies were rated according to the degree to which they were being directed to each of the five problem areas; problem areas were then compared with the ratings of cost factors described above. The resulting associations are summarized in Table 4.2, showing the typical use of various resources given the types of problems being addressed.

Recruitment, training, and supervision costs were relatively high when program strategies were directed to problems requiring material assistance, help with finding housing or jobs, and needs for personal advocacy. The costs were not typically as high when the focus was on neighborhood affairs or community development. Staff coordination of helper tasks or of different helpers appeared to be a common practice, although not to the same degree for all problems. Agencies devoting more attention to clients with multiple problems or chronic conditions tended to assign a greater number of staff FTE to the program, although the average percentage of time of each staff member was not typically high. Neighborhood problems required fewer staff FTE in work with helpers, although the average staff member had a greater percentage of time allocated to this activity out of their overall agency responsibilities. The staff spent more time on unstructured activities with helpers when the focus of their work was on either clients' needs for community adjustment or broader neighborhood issues. Time spent on unstructured contacts with helpers was also typical for chronic problems that overburden the family. Payment of helpers occurred most often when they provided material assistance or personal advocacy. Mechanisms for coordination among staff were emphasized in situations dealing with chronic or multiple problems, perhaps because these problems involved greater allocation of total staff FTE but a lesser proportion of each individual staff member's time. Finally, backup services

TABLE 4.2 Association between Cost Factors and Problem Focus

Cost Factor	needs for material assistance, jobs housing	individual rights personal advocacy	community adjustment, activities daily living, social support	multiple problems, chronic conditions, family burden	neighborhood affairs, community problems
Supervisory					
● staff supervision of helpers	++	++	+	0	0
● staff responsibility for helper activities	++	++	0	0	0
● staff coordination of helper activities	++	++	+	+	+
Recruitment and Training					
● formal recruitment activities employed	+	++	0	0	0
● formal training provided	++	++	0	+	0
Staff Effort					
● greater number of staff FTE	+	+	+	++	0
● greater % of staff time allocated to working with helpers	+	0	0	0	+
● extent to which unstructured time is spent with helper	0	0	++	+	++
Payment					
● helpers provided stipend or reimbursed	++	++	0	0	0
Coordination					
● need for coordination among staff in working with helpers	+	0	0	++	0
Backup					
● need for professional or agency services as backup to helper activities	+	0	+	+	0

KEY: ++ VERY TYPICAL
      + SOMEWHAT TYPICAL
      0 NOT TYPICAL

were emphasized in all problem areas except those addressing neighborhood problems or problems needing personal advocacy. For these problems, the helper activities were directed less to providing services directly and more to issues of availability of services in other agencies in the community or to problems such as neighborhood improvement which did not require client services.

Overall, cost factors varied according to the type of problems being addressed. Where there was a need for personalized, emotional, or ongoing involvement between helpers, clients, and staff, greater amounts of staff time were required. Problems requiring special skills or knowledge (providing advocacy or obtaining material resources) required greater investments in recruiting, training, supervision, or payment of helpers.

COST OF PROGRAM STRATEGIES

Thus far, we have examined the prevalence of various cost factors on an agency-wide basis. Costs also can be expected to vary with respect to the particular strategies or combinations of strategies an agency has employed to work with informal helpers. Each strategy differs in terms of its problem focus, the number of helpers involved, and the demands made on agency staff. To identify the "package" of costs associated with different strategies, we compared the prevalence of the various cost factors for each agency with the extent to which the agency employed one or more of the five types of program strategies discussed earlier. The resulting associations are displayed in Table 4.3, showing the degree to which various costs were incurred by employing each approach. Each strategy differs substantially in the range of cost factors required for its implementation, largely as a function of the types and numbers of helpers involved and the nature of the relationship developed between staff and helpers. We will discuss each strategy in turn.

The personal network strategy usually involves an individual staff member working on a one-to-one basis with clients and informally involving the client's network of significant others in the provision of care. Therefore, costs associated with recruitment, training, and supervision were absent, since helpers within the client's network provide assistance on the basis of their established relationship with the client. For the same reason, helpers were not paid. More staff effort was involved in this approach because each client generally

TABLE 4.3   Association Between Cost Factors and Type of Strategies Utilized

Cost Factor	Personal Network	Volunteer Linking	Mutual Aid	Neighborhood Helping	Community Empowerment
Supervisory					
• staff supervision of helpers	0	++	0	0	0
• staff responsibility for helper activities	0	++	+	0	0
• staff coordination of helper activities	0	++	0	+	+
Recruitment and Training					
• formal recruitment activities employed	0	++	0	0	0
• formal training provided	0	++	0	0	0
Staff Effort					
• greater # of staff FTE	+	+	+	0	0
• greater % of staff time allocated to working with helpers	+	0	+	0	+
• extent to which staff spend unstructured time with helpers	+	0	0	++	++
Payment					
• helpers provided stipend or reimbursed	0	+	0	0	0
Coordination					
• need for coordination among staff in working with helpers	++	0	0	+	+
Backup					
• need for professional or agency services as backup to helper activities	+	+	++	0	0

KEY: ++ VERY TYPICAL
        + SOMEWHAT TYPICAL
        0 NOT TYPICAL

had several people with whom the staff were in contact. There were also likely to be unstructured, ad hoc expenditures of time which grew as the size of the staff member's caseload increased. Although individual staff members had separate client caseloads, the need for staff coordination to obtain support and feedback on their work was reportedly high among the agencies which employed this strategy. The strategy was usually employed in conjunction with backup services which supplemented all the various forms of assistance given by helpers in the client's network of family, friends, and neighbors.

The volunteer linking strategy displayed a contrasting set of cost factors. This strategy involved the identification of lay helpers, previously unknown by the client, and the development of a dyadic relationship between the volunteer helper and the client to address the client's special needs for advocacy, companionship, or counseling. The tasks performed by these helpers usually required special skills and a considerable investment of time, and thus the costs of recruitment, training, and supervision were greater. Payment of helpers was more often employed, either in the form of a stipend or a reimbursement for the helper's out-of-pocket expenses while working with clients. Staff spent less time with helpers and the need for coordination among staff was less due to the greater specificity or explicitness of helper roles and responsibilities. The strategy was generally used in conjunction with other services in the agency, so that backup services were in some instances an additional necessary investment.

The mutual aid network strategy connected staff with existing mutual aid groups or created networks among clients or people with similar interests to promote sharing of personal concerns and experiences. In this context, helpers were usually people within the network who played key roles in sustaining network activities or fostering member participation. Aside from situations where staff initiated the development of mutual aid networks and thus needed to take some initial responsibility for activities, the costs associated with recruitment, training, and supervision were generally absent in this strategy. More staff effort was sometimes necessary if the network was very large. The strategy usually was integrated into other agency services both for backup services and as a way to recruit members for the network.

The major costs associated with the next two strategies, neighborhood helping and community empowerment, were those that related to the amount of staff time devoted to informal contact with helpers. Informal contact involved staff spending time in the neighborhood or community, chatting with people on the street to learn more about local issues and leaders, or visiting individual helpers to develop a relationship. Staff also devoted time to coordinating the activities of different helpers, as well as coordinating with each other to make sure needed information was exchanged about mutual contacts, events in the community, or other activities that staff members may have attended separately. Other costs involving supervision, formal recruitment, and training were relatively absent, as helpers were usually encountered on their own territory and performed tasks independently.

Although certain strategies (e.g., mutual aid) incurred fewer overall costs, one must remember that different strategies also addressed different types of objectives, tasks, and activities. Thus, it is not useful to look for the cheapest way of working with informal helpers since these other considerations will play a large part in determining which strategy to choose. More specialized tasks, greater involvement of helpers in client services, and more difficult problems requiring the availability of professional services were elements which were likely to increase the costliness of any strategy. To the extent that several strategies could be combined or integrated within the procedures of other services the agency provided, however, there were likely to be overall cost savings. As we discuss in the next chapter, helpers participated in more than one strategy in many programs. They helped clients of the agency who were part of their personal network, participated in several local community groups, and volunteered at the agency as well. This kind of flexibility of roles among helpers can be of particular benefit in linking clients with different aspects of community life, as well as increasing the interaction of the agency with consumers and other community members. It can also result in saving staff time in recruitment, coordination, and communication of information.

Consequences

The costs of working with informal helpers, whether presented in qualitative terms or hard dollar figures, have little meaning unless there is also some picture of the types and extent of beneficial consequences that can be expected to result from adopting alternative strategies.

The main goals the thirty agencies expected to achieve were more responsiveness to clients and greater efficiency in service delivery. They believed that mutual participation among providers, consumers, and significant others in the determination of needs and the joint use of professional and informal resources would result in a more appropriate response to problems along with a more sparing application of scarce agency resources.

To be sure, the manner in which these goals were translated into program objectives varied with the issues relevant to the particular populations being served and with the configuration of services each agency was able to provide. For those working with the elderly, informal helpers were seen as reducing social isolation, helping to sustain the elderly person in the community, and enhancing the psychological and emotional status of the client. For those working with the disabled (either developmentally, physically, or mentally), helpers were seen as promoting community adjustment, reducing dependency, and promoting self-sufficiency. Agencies concerned with the problems of children, youth, and families involved informal helpers to increase the responsiveness of services to clients, to strengthen the capacity of informal resources, and to promote family social integration. Agencies directing staff energies to the general community saw the informal participation of citizen helpers as essential for the promotion of local control and community self-determination.

Underlying the specific consequences expected by each agency of their work with informal helpers were eight generic criteria for assessing outcomes. Agencies used informal helpers to make positive impacts in the areas shown in Table 4.4: accessibility, responsiveness, client satisfaction, use of informal resources, self-sufficiency, service efficiency, community control, and reduction in clients being institutionalized. The agencies in the sample did not place an equal emphasis on each of these criteria. The range of consequences suggested by the eight criteria represent common expectations shared by most of the staff in their work with informal helpers.

The extent to which these criteria were met by the efforts of agency staff quite naturally varied given the relevance of each consequence to program goals and objectives and the mix of strategies employed. A number of agencies had formally assessed impacts in several of the areas and had evidence on the nature and extent of consequences of their work with informal helpers. These evaluation studies illustrate the range of results:

- A program in Manhattan working with the personal networks of elderly clients to promote the maintenance of clients in the community

TABLE 4.4   Generic Outcome Criteria for Assessing Partnerships

Accessibility
- availability of an adequate range of alternative services
- cultural and psychological acceptability of service provision
- geographical and psychological accessibility of services

Responsiveness
- targeting services to special needs or population groups
- awareness of rights to services
- responsiveness of mandated services to client's needs

Client Satisfaction and Well Being
- client satisfaction with services
- emotional and psychological status

Self-Sufficiency
- self-determination in the definition and resolution of client problems
- self-sufficiency in economic and social resources
- reduced dependency on formal services

Use of Informal Resources
- use of informal care in meeting needs
- reduction in need for formal services

Deinstitutionalization
- reduction of hospitalization or institutional care
- reduction in social isolation of clients

Efficiency
- range of services offered with existing staff resources
- cost/unit of services
- cost/client

Local Control
- participation of community residents in determination of program services
- community voice in decision-making about local affairs

reported improved client satisfaction, enhanced emotional and psychological status, and significant postponement of needs for institutionalization (Zimmer, 1978);

- A program in San Diego that employed strategies of supporting helpers in an elderly client's personal network and involvement in mutual aid activities among neighborhood elderly found evidence of improved client satisfaction, reduced isolation, and increased mobility (Toseland, Decker & Bliesner, 1979);

- A two-year controlled study of a program in Benton, Illinois, that employed a combination of strategies in working with the elderly including an emphasis on involving the client's significant others, encouraging neighborhood helpers, and developing mutual aid activities reported improved client well-being, improved responsiveness of mandated services to clients, and 50 percent reduction of elderly clients being institutionalized (Ehrlich, 1979);

- A three-year study of a program in Arkansas which made extensive use of lay helpers in addressing the problem of child abuse and neglect found in comparing the program with a dozen other programs being studied nationally that the lay helper approach was substantially more cost effective in reducing client recidivism (Berkeley Planning Associates, 1977);

- A follow-up study of clients in a Houston program working to promote independent living opportunities for the severely disabled through the use of disabled and able-bodied lay volunteers and through mutual aid reported increased client well-being and self-sufficiency, improved physical functioning and mobility, and progress in meeting vocational and educational objectives (Cole & Frieden, 1977);

- A controlled, follow-up study of clients of a program in Tampa working with chronic mental patients by involving client helpers and mutual aid found improved client well-being and 50 percent reduction in recidivism rates, reduced hospital days for those who were institutionalized, and a 50 percent reduction in the use of community services (Edmonson, Bedell & Gordon, 1980);

- A study of a community development program in Durham, North Carolina, which made extensive use of neighborhood helpers reported improved accessibility and responsiveness of services to community residents (Joyner, 1978);

- Programs in Milwaukee and Chicago working with neighborhood helpers and mutual aid activities report increased participation, satisfaction, and self-sufficiency among residents (Andrews & Norton, 1979; Biegel & Naparstek, 1979).

Not all of the thirty agencies in our sample were able to provide documented evidence to suggest the degree to which potential consequences were in fact actual consequences. For many agencies, evidence of impact was more qualitative, relying on specific case examples, progress reports, and staff experiences. This type of evidence points to a probable impact although one not systematically documented. In other cases the evidence was indirect, since it was

less feasible to demonstrate direct impacts for criteria such as
responsiveness or self-determination. The impact in these cases was
possible, but not demonstrated. Finally, there are a number of
instances where it was unlikely that expectations for obtaining
certain consequences would be met either because program strategies
were difficult to implement or because staff or helper efforts did not
significantly address a particular objective.

To appreciate the extent to which consequences within the eight
areas of impact criteria could be expected from the agency's work
with informal helpers, program evidence was assessed to determine
whether potential consequences were in fact *documented* by systematic study, *probable* given qualitative reports, *possible* but not
demonstrated, *unlikely* or *not relevant* to agency goals and objectives. This approach to assessing outcomes has certain limitations.
First, the ratings will reflect the *probability* that certain outcomes
will be achieved. In part, this will be determined by the extent to
which staff have formally tried to take account of the consequences
of their work. Thus, agencies not concerned about demonstrating
effects will receive lower ratings. Second, the ratings will also reflect
the *emphasis* given to various outcome objectives by staff in their
work. Outcome areas that staff do not view as relevant to their work
or that are given low priority will be rated lower. Thus, the rating will
show when a given outcome can be *demonstrated* to have occurred.
However, a lower rating does not necessarily indicate that an
outcome did not in fact occur, but simply that it was not demonstrated
or emphasized by agency staff. This interpretation of the outcome
assessments should be kept in mind in later discussions. The
resulting distribution of assessments within each generic outcome
area for the thirty agencies is shown in Table 4.5.

In four outcome areas—accessibility, use of informal resources,
deinstitutionalization, and local control—almost one-fifth of the
thirty agencies have documented evidence of program impact. If we
include both documented and probable evidence, more than half of
the programs show program impact for all criteria except client self-
sufficiency. To some extent, this may be a more stringent criterion
insofar as self-sufficiency requires improvements in economic status
or physical functioning, objectives which may require substantial
efforts by staff and helpers for clients with difficult problems. This
area along with the areas of efficiency and local control were not seen
as relevant to stated program objectives by a number of programs.

TABLE 4.5   Distribution of Generic Outcomes Among Agencies (N = 30)

CRITERIA	*not applicable*	*unlikely*	*possible*	*probable*	*documented*
		Reported Outcome			
Accessibility • improved availability, acceptibility, and accessibility of services to client	0	3	6	17	4
Responsiveness • improved responsiveness of mandated services to clients, targeting of special needs and awareness of services	1	2	12	15	0
Client Satisfaction and Well-Being • improved client satisfaction with services and enhanced psychological/emotional status	0	1	5	21	3
Self Sufficiency • increase in economic and physical self-sufficiency; reduction in dependency	3	12	11	3	1
Use of Informal Resources • increased use of informal care and reduced need for services	0	5	6	14	5
Deinstitutionalization • reduction of institutionalization and social isolation	0	4	8	12	6
Efficiency • more efficient use of available staff resources; reduced cost/unit or cost/client	4	7	5	12	2
Local Control • increase in community participation and local control of programs	3	3	5	12	7

Overall, the strength of impact in the generic outcome areas provides positive evidence of the scope of consequences that can be expected from professional collaboration with informal sources of care.

THE CONSEQUENCES OF ALTERNATIVE PROGRAM STRATEGIES

This global picture of the distribution of outcomes needs to be refined according to the types of strategies staff employ in their work. To address this level of analysis, the impacts of each program were compared with the extent to which they employed the five alternative strategies described earlier. Table 4.6 shows the resulting distribution of associations between program strategies and outcome levels.

Each strategy exhibits a different pattern of outcome. The personal network strategy is relatively strong in improving accessibility, availability, and acceptability of services, probably because of the more intimate and personal involvement of staff with each client's family and social ties. As noted in several of the studies cited earlier, the strategy also exhibited strength in reducing isolation and institutionalization. This impact probably reflects the emphasis this approach puts on family involvement, since other research indicates that family rejection and burden is a common reason for institutionalization (Kreissman & Joy, 1974).

The volunteer linking strategy was most often directed to the needs of a disabled population in the agencies in our sample. In our analysis, the strategy was shown to have greater impact in the areas of improved self-sufficiency, increased use of informal resources, and increased program efficiency. Many of the needs of the disabled population involve assistance with activities of daily living, community adjustment, and socialization. It is likely that the availability of a dyadic relationship with a volunteer helper as a friendly companion and advocate is an efficient means of addressing these needs without the use of more specialized professional resources.

The mutual aid network strategy adopted by the majority of the thirty agencies worked well in achieving beneficial consequences in three areas: client satisfaction and well-being, use of informal resources, and deinstitutionalization. By linking together individuals with common needs and shared concerns, greater use was made of the client's own resources. Social interaction was promoted among individuals who had similar experiences. It is likely that the mutual understanding and acceptance of problems by the group improved

TABLE 4.6   Association Between Generic Outcome Strategies

	STRATEGY				
Criteria	*Personal Network*	*Volunteer Linking*	*Mutual Aid Network*	*Neighborhood Helpers*	*Community Empowerment*
Accessibility • improved availability, acceptability, and accessibility of services to clients	++	0	0	+	+
Responsiveness • improved responsiveness of mandated services to clients, targeting of special needs and awareness of services	+	0	+	0	+
Client Satisfaction and Well-Being • improved client satisfaction with services and enhanced psychological/emotional status	0	0	++	0	++
Self Sufficiency • increase in self-determination, self-sufficiency, reduction in dependency	+	++	+	0	++
Use of Informal Resources • increased use of informal care and reduced need for services	+	++	++	+	++
Institutionalization • reduction of institutionalization and social isolation	++	+	++	0	0
Efficiency • more efficient use of available staff resources; reduced cost/unit or cost/client	+	++	+	+	0
Local Control • increase in community participation and local control of programs	0	0	+	++	++

KEY: ++ VERY TYPICAL
         + SOMEWHAT TYPICAL
         0 NOT TYPICAL

the psychological and emotional status of participants (Lieberman, Borman & Associates, 1977). Because the strategy focused on issues and problems internal to a given mutual aid group, it had less impact on outcome criteria that reflect a broader scope of issues—for example, improved responsiveness of and access to services.

The last two strategies, neighborhood helping and community empowerment, involved individuals in activities that often were not directly client-focused. As such, many of the client-related outcome criteria were assessed more indirectly and thus do not show a particularly strong association. Both strategies had their strongest impact in the area of improving local control through increasing community participation and neighborhood involvement. Both made favorable impacts on increasing the use of informal resources in meeting needs. The community empowerment approach showed strength in the areas of improving client satisfaction and well-being and increasing self-sufficiency. This was probably because the agencies employed this approach in conjunction with several other approaches more specifically directed to clients. The connection between services to individual clients and broader community participation and neighborhood integration seemed to enhance the well-being and self-sufficiency of program participants.

A more integrated picture of each approach is given in Table 4.7, which presents a composite profile of each strategy, based on agency experiences, outlining the range of problems typically addressed by that specific strategy, the types of costs associated with each strategy, and the range of consequences that can be expected from it.

Summary and Discussion

The analysis of costs and consequences associated with the ways agency staff have sought to interweave professional care with informal sources of help reveals a rather complex picture of what can be expected, but one which holds significant promise for improving service delivery to a wide range of target populations. Summarizing the major findings, the analysis has supported a number of important conclusions:

(1) The costs of adopting the alternative approaches primarily involved changes in agency practices rather than direct financial outlay. These costs included: use of staff time, use of facilities, donated time and facilities, some resources for payment or reim-

TABLE 4.7 Summary of Costs and Consequences of Program Strategies

Strategy	Problems Addressed	Costs Involved	Consequences
PERSONAL NETWORK	• multiple problems, chronic • some adjustment, skills of daily living problems • less material assistance, housing, employment problems • not used in relation to advocacy, individual rights or neighborhood related problems	• usually more staff involved (FTE) • greater staff effort devoted to approach (% time) • backup services may or may not be necessary depending on problem • supervision costs not necessary • more staff coordination • greater use of nonprofessional staff • payment of helpers rare, if at all	• demonstrable reduction in institutionalization of clients • improved accessibility, acceptability and availability of services possible • prevention of needs for service likely • improvement in self-determination and self-sufficiency likely • may increase efficiency in use of existing resources
VOLUNTEER LINKING	• more problems related to personal advocacy, stigma • some problems needing material assistance • may be directed to problems involving community adjustment or chronic problems • not used in relation to neighborhood problems	• supervisory costs are often involved including costs associated with identifying, recruiting, training and supervising helpers • usually does not require large number of staff (FTE) or large proportion of staff time (% time) • backup services sometimes made available • payment (either stipend or reimbursement) is sometimes offered • less need for staff coordination • less use of nonprofessional staff	• demonstrable improvement in efficiency by lowering cost per unit of service or cost/client • demonstrable increase in client self-sufficiency • some reduction of institutionalization possible • may increase use of informal resources • may increase responsiveness of mandated services to clients

(continued)

103

TABLE 4.7 Summary of Costs and Consequences of Program Strategies (continued)

Strategy	Problems Addressed	Costs Involved	Consequences
MUTUAL AID NETWORKS	• most often used in conjunction with needs of community adjustment, activities of daily living, social support	• few supervisory costs are involved, especially involving identification, training or coordination; staff may need to assume more responsibility for activities involving populations with chronic problems	• improved client satisfaction, psychological and emotional status probable
			• greater use of informal resources reported
	• some use with chronic problems as a supplemental approach	• may use more staff members (FTE) although staff effort (% time) may be less	• reduction of institutionalization or needs for services documented in some cases
		• less need for staff coordination	• improved self-sufficiency
		• backup services are usually required	• may improve efficiency by offering more services with existing resources
		• payment (either stipend or reimbursement) may sometimes be utilized for helpers who take on greater responsibility	
NEIGHBORHOOD HELPERS	• most often used in relation to problems of community adjustment, neighborhood affairs where client population can be addressed through area of residence	• may use nonprofessional staff	
		• few supervisory costs are involved in training, direct supervision; staff time coordinating helpers may be necessary	• improvement in accessibility probable
			• more use of local resources reported
	• some use in relation to assistance with activities of daily living (e.g., elderly)	• usually requires fewer staff FTE	• greater self-sufficiency possible
		• more staff time spent on informal canvassing, contacting; less staff responsibility for helper activities	• greater responsiveness to special needs when used in conjunction with other approaches

(continued)

TABLE 4.7 Summary of Costs and Consequences of Program Strategies (continued)

Strategy	Problems Addressed	Costs Involved	Consequences
	• little or no use in connection with problems associated with personal advocacy, individual rights	• backup services not usually required • payment of helpers rare • more coordination time among staff may be necessary • may use nonprofessional staff	• some efficiency gains reported when approach used as supplement to client services
COMMUNITY EMPOWERMENT	• most often directed to neighborhood problems dealing with issues of community development, planning appropriate services • some use in connection with advocacy for particular constituencies in community • less directed to problems associated with individual clients although approach may be employed in conjunction with other strategies to deal with client problems	• supervisory costs associated with coordination among helpers; few costs associated with training or supervision of helper activities • usually less staff FTE and % time involved in approach • less need for backup services • nonprofessionals sometimes employed as staff • greater need for staff coordination • payment of helpers rare • more staff time spent informally contacting or working with helpers	• improvement in local community control of services • responsiveness to target populations, special needs improved; increase in responsiveness of mandated services • greater use of existing informal resources probable • improvement in client self-sufficiency and satisfaction with services when approach is used in conjunction with other strategies directed to clients

bursement of helpers, and general administrative and overhead costs.

(2) Costs of any sort were relatively minimal:

- most programs employed fewer than five staff FTE; one-third of the programs used only one or two staff;
- almost half of the programs used staff less than full time in work with informal helpers;
- most helpers were unpaid and untrained;
- paraprofessionals were often employed in place of professional staff in work with the informal helpers;
- overhead and facility costs varied by the extent to which the agency incorporated the approach into existing services and was able to utilize existing facilities in the community.

(3) Costs involving staff time, recruiting, training, and coordinating or supervising helpers, providing payment, or providing for internal staff coordination and backup services were greater when the following problems or tasks were involved:

- specialized client needs or problems that involved chronic burden;
- tasks that required special knowledge or skills regarding problems and available services;
- tasks that required staff to spend time canvassing the community, contacting helpers, and maintaining informal relationships.

(4) The consequences of the alternative approaches adopted by the thirty agencies varied by the particular problems and objectives of the agency but included outcomes related to client status, agency provision of service, intra-agency relations, and community-wide issues.

(5) Many of the effects of the strategies for working with informal sources of care were difficult to measure and most programs had not made systematic assessments of outcome. However, about one-third of the programs had documented evidence, often from controlled studies, to demonstrate the effectiveness of alternative approaches. This suggests that systematic program evaluation is possible but not always feasible.

(6) Programs have attributed a wide number of outcomes to their work with informal helpers including:

- increased accessibility and responsiveness of services;
- increased cost efficiency and use of informal resources in meeting needs;
- reduction in institutionalization of clients;
- increased local participation and control in service delivery.

These findings point to the potential benefits of adopting strategies for interweaving formal and informal sources of care. Yet it must be realized that the analysis is exploratory, and that major limitations argue for caution in interpreting the findings. The sample of agencies is not random or representative, but purposive in order to explore the range of problems, strategies, and settings, and to suggest areas which may merit further investigation. Agency documentation and staff interviews formed the base of information for making assessments. The possibility of overstatement or bias cannot be ruled out, although some agencies have been able to provide rigorous evidence. Many of the programs in our sample were relatively small, sometimes no more than a storefront agency with one or two staff. It is unclear whether their experiences will apply to larger agencies, although there were a number of such agencies included in the study that had incorporated similar efforts into their operations. Finally, this analysis comprises a qualitative evaluation of the costs and consequences associated with different strategies. Thus, our conclusions must be tempered by the realization that more systematic program demonstration and research are needed in order to assess actual costs and consequences and to determine whether the findings can be replicated with different populations and within different agencies.

There are elements missing from the analysis that also condition the findings. As noted at the outset, the "externalities" of adopting the alternative strategies must be examined. Questions to be answered include: How much does the increased use of informal resources to solve problems undermine individual access to needed services and potentially increase family burden? How much does promoting local awareness and involvement actually increase the demand for services on the system as a whole? Is the help provided by family, friends, neighbors, or mutual aid groups of the same quality or kind as professional care? We will return to these issues in the final chapter.

On balance, the analysis provides enough evidence to warrant support for efforts by formal agencies and professional service providers to link up with and involve informal caregivers, whether family and friends, neighborhood helpers, mutual aid networks, or neighborhood associations, in the design and provision of services. Our findings are also amplified by the work of others which document that approaches for collaboration exist, have been successfully implemented in a number of situations, and offer substantial benefits in improving service delivery (see Bayley, 1978; President's Commission on Mental Health, 1978 for reviews).

Chapter 5

COMBINING PROGRAM STRATEGIES

In the last two chapters we have discussed each of the alternative program strategies employed by agencies, focusing on various aspects of staff procedures and agency implementation as well as attendant costs and consequences. While each of the five strategies for working with different types of informal helping networks can be conceptually outlined as a separate strategy, it should be emphasized that in practice they are usually not considered by staff as independent from other activities undertaken within the agency. Also, most strategies worked best when other formal services were available to supplement the help which the informal system is able to provide.

In this chapter we outline several of the more popular combinations of program strategies employed by the agencies in our study. Case examples are presented to illustrate how combinations may work in specific situations. Following the presentation of examples, we discuss the benefits of combined strategies.

Case Illustrations

Only a minority of agencies in our study worked with informal helping networks in just one way. In these instances, either the mutual aid or the neighborhood helping strategies were employed singularly. Usually, staff conceived of the strategies as being mutually reinforcing because they provided opportunities for the tasks of care and support to be distributed among a broader range of social relationships. For example, because the volunteer linking approach emphasizes the development of separate dyadic relationships between clients and volunteer helpers, agency staff often combined it with a mutual aid strategy in order to expand the range of a client's social contacts. Similarly, since the personal network approach emphasizes an individual's existing set of social ties, which are often limited for clients who have severe problems or are socially isolated, many agencies used the mutual aid strategy to enlist additional support resources either for the clients or for caregivers in the network. The neighborhood helper strategy was often integrated into work with the client's personal network and mutual aid activities. Finally, agencies using the community empowerment approach also employed other client-related strategies in order to address needs identified by the community in service planning, and to strengthen the role of the community's own resources in serving local client needs.

These combinations outline the possibilities and indicate the rationale behind coordinated strategies; several case examples will illustrate in more detail how these combinations can be put into practice. For example, an agency serving the elderly illustrates the use of the mutual aid and neighborhood helping strategies in tandem:

The program serves those who are 60 years old or older and live in two census tracts, with the aim of extending mutual aid and self-help among the elderly in the neighborhood. The program is staffed by a program coordinator, three social workers, a nurse, and a nurse's aide, in addition to an evaluation team. The major effort of the program has been to organize elderly volunteers from the area into task forces to provide services to their neighbors. The home maintenance task force provides home repair, gardening and yard work, and housecleaning; the home health task force has groups which provide friendly visiting and telephone reassurance as well as self-help groups for those with arthritis, diabetes, and hypertension; and the social service task force provides information and assistance in acquiring social services, education, recreation, and therapy classes as well as programs to "maintain and sustain" the volunteers.

Much of the mutual aid activity occurs in groups. For example, friendly visiting groups meet three times a week and go in pairs to visit people in the area. Home repair and maintenance is also usually carried out by a team. Volunteers also associate with each other regularly at the nearby nutrition center, at task force and advisory council meetings, and through activities planned for the volunteers as incentives. Over time, relationships among volunteers and with those they help often turn into friendship, increasing the network of ties and potential for additional mutual aid within the neighborhood.

[*Case No. 9*]

Another example shows how the personal network, mutual aid, and neighborhood helping strategies can be integrated to expand the range of social opportunities and social support available to clients. The illustration comes from an elderly services program that operates out of a senior center in a small town.

The program model is neighborhood-based and encourages mutual help among neighbors. The mutual help model is based on the premise that people can and do help themselves and others, that people (including the elderly) can identify their own needs and can organize to meet those needs primarily through their own efforts. The neighbor-helping-neighbor approach opens up or revitalizes the roles of neighbor and friend, and creates potential roles as a member of the neighborhood group and as community activist or consumer spokesperson. The small town has been divided up into ten smaller areas or "neighborhoods." All the elderly in each of these neighborhoods have been identified by name and street, and all have been invited to participate in the closest neighborhood group for the elderly. The groups meet twice a month, primarily for social and recreational activities with some added elements—blood pressures are taken, information about services, programs and special events, and about other elderly individuals in the neighborhood are shared. The group participants are encouraged to reach out to their home-bound and hospitalized neighbors.

Often elderly persons call the agency with specific problems or needs. The community aide works with that individual to find persons who have been helpful in the past and from whom the individual is willing to accept help for this particular problem. These are frequently elderly neighbors, friends, family members, or church members. The aide encourages the individual to seek appropriate help from this personal network, and the aide also checks in with these persons about their perceptions of the situation and their willingness and ability to respond. Staff monitor the efficacy of the help available to the individual from this personal network.

Similarly, the community aides work informally with key community resources for the elderly. They encourage storekeepers, doctors, and clergymen to be sensitive to the needs of the elderly and to modify their services in ways that make them more accessible and appropriate to the elderly.

The role of the community aide in this neighborhood-based service approach is to activate peer networks among the elderly by encouraging neighbors to help neighbors, to increase the visibility and accessibility of existing formal service programs for the elderly, and to act as advocates and educators within the elderly population, the community, and other service agencies for improving the formal services for the elderly.

[*Case No. 1*]

An alternative set of strategies combines volunteer linking and mutual aid. This combination was often used by agencies dealing with clients with difficult problems (e.g., developmentally or physically disabled; child-abuse families). Here, the support provided on a one-to-one basis by a volunteer helper is supplemented by a mutual aid support network in order to share the potential burden that difficult problems might present. An agency serving the developmentally disabled illustrates how the combination may be implemented with a view toward providing a "personal advocacy system" for clients:

The personal advocacy system is comprised of four major parts: citizen advocacy, consumer rights, self-advocacy, and parent advocacy. The citizen advocacy component has the objectives of providing for the personal and advocacy needs of disabled individuals through one-to-one matches between citizen volunteers and developmentally disabled persons; and since 1973 it has grown in size, coverage, and sophistication. More than a hundred active volunteers have become involved, and the component functions both in the community and in the state hospital to link disabled individuals with personal advocates. As the longest standing service of the agency, the process of making successful matches has been refined from experience and has pointed to the need for other advocacy services.

The consumer rights component was added later to deal with the need to inform disabled individuals, their families, and other service providers of the legal, educational, and service rights that have been established by law. A representative provides paralegal counseling and advocacy, often working with other agencies to ensure the appropriateness and accessibility of mandated services.

The self-advocacy program provides counseling, assertiveness training, and group meetings to assist disabled persons to advocate for
themselves. The program operates in conjunction with People First, a
self-help group, and has several groups involving about twenty to
thirty individuals living in the community and about fifty who reside in
the state hospital.

Beginning in 1977, the parent advocacy component was started. The
program was originally conceived as a program in which parents of
recently identified children with a developmental disability would be
matched with other parents who had gone through a similar experience
and were willing and able to provide support and counsel to new
parents in adjusting to new demands. The concept has since been
expanded to include a more comprehensive view of parent advocacy
incorporating both an emphasis on parents helping parents as well as
the parent's role in advocating in the community for the larger needs of
the developmentally disabled population. This led to the creation of a
Parents Advocacy Council which grew out of the existing networks
among parents in the community and has, in turn, created other
networks of mutual aid and advocacy.

[*Case No. 16*]

The final case illustration is more extended and comes from a
neighborhood-based multiservice agency. Located in an urban,
multiethnic neighborhood with mixed social classes, the agency was
quite innovative in integrating most of the alternative strategies in the
context of serving a variety of different target populations. Agency
staff had developed an integrated perspective on the nature of
different helping networks:

In providing direct services to individuals, staff attempt to identify
and work with the personal network of a client and enlist family,
friends, and neighbors in providing assistance. In many situations
where an existing network is not available to help out, the client is
linked to others with similar problems or concerns. Staff have often
worked to develop mutual aid networks or formalize self-help groups
for this purpose. Staff efforts to organize mutual aid groups take two
forms, and it is here that the integration between client and community
work occurs. In situations where meeting a client's needs for an
intimate and trusting relationship is the objective, informal and
loosely organized groups will be developed. Where the group has the
potential for adopting a community wide focus, staff efforts are
directed to developing a more organized and ultimately independent

and self-sufficient organization that may have a voice in community affairs. Other strategies for creating community-wide networks include using the media, conducting issue forums, and extensive canvassing and on-the-street contacting of residents. All these staff efforts are directed to promoting self-reliance by taking such roles as informal colleague, task facilitator, and others. To the extent possible, staff oversee moving a client from dependency to personal autonomy and on to community participation and involvement. In this way, staff see their work with clients and the neighborhood as inseparable.

With such a conceptual base, the agency's staff are involved with a complex array of helping networks in four program components that are directed to youth, seniors, family social services, and community development. What is unique is the extent to which there is overlapping and coordination of services among the separate components and the networks each fosters. Because of this complexity, the inclusion of helping networks within services can be more clearly presented by describing selected illustrations followed by a listing of other relevant examples to indicate the breadth of the application of network concepts to services.

Youth: The development of ties to a juvenile gang of Chicano youth illustrates one major way the program has enlisted an existing network for helping purposes. The program began to recruit gangleaders to work as agency staff in order to draw delinquent youth into the program and provide peer-oriented problem-solving. Five peer leaders were recruited by extensive interviews and hired for paid positions. Training in counseling and community resources was provided, but the essential character of the peer leader's role relied upon their reputation and knowledge of the youth subculture within the neighborhood. Peer workers are supervised as regular staff and are included in the decision-making within the agency.

This component also has created or enlisted several other types of networks: a youth advisory board of about six local youth who provide input to a city council member on youth-related issues; a parents' advisory board of about 12 individuals created among the parents of youth clients to get them involved in services for youth 6 to 13 years old; and a child-care exchange network which was developed on a block level.

Senior Services: The core of this component also adopts a peer worker approach by employing four elderly paraprofessionals to provide counseling, information and referral, and a range of other kinds of assistance. In addition to their ties to and knowledge of the neighborhood which help to link elderly clients into existing networks, senior service workers also employ a more structured approach to networking in the course of counseling. In particular, clients are asked to chart their personal networks upon referral; this chart is kept in the client's file with a major effort directed to helping the client plan ways to expand this natural support system. This is done through contacting old friends or forgotten ties, social activities in senior clubs or religious institutions, and other opportunities to make social contacts.

The effectiveness of personal network intervention is aided by several other activities of the program. A full time outreach worker directs attention to canvassing elderly neighborhoods, friendly visiting, and working with residents of a forty-unit senior complex. Through these efforts, a telephone reassurance network has been set up among elderly shut-ins and key neighborhood helpers have been linked to elderly citizens. Another illustration of the program's emphasis on mutual aid networks can be found in the Senior Neighbors Club, a self-help network developed by agency staff. The association functions independently of the program now but often joins in program activities and serves as a referral for linking elderly clients into neighborhood activities.

Social Services: This component works with families (many of which are single parent) and single adults and provides a wide range of counseling, crisis, employment, and advocacy services. Because of the difficulties of many of the multiproblem families, basic needs are often the focus of services. Yet, this component shares the emphasis on self-reliance and mutual aid found in other components. In addition to attempting to develop neighborhood links with helpers and creating women and single parent support groups, social services use a "value for value" concept. As a way to improve a client's self-esteem, clients are often asked to reciprocate by providing assistance to others in return for help received, or giving something of value for value received. For example, one male client assisted in painting the office after he had been helped by the staff. Clients may make lists of the various types of help they can provide to be called upon later when another may need such help. This is also a way to increase a client's social involvement in the neighborhood community.

Community Development: Perhaps the most notable outcome of staff work in this component has been the formalization and official recognition of the Planning Council, which grew out of a loosely affiliated network of residents staff had organized around the issue of land use planning and redevelopment in the neighborhood. Now, the Planning Council is a free standing entity with members formally elected and with a charter from the city council to review and approve development within the neighborhood. The community development component also has sponsored the development of a bilingual neighborhood-based newspaper, with stories often written by community residents. The newspaper serves both as a way to involve community members in the neighborhood and as a tool for linking people to others.

A more recent effort is the Neighborhood Awareness Project, which is illustrative of the application of network ideas to community organizations. The program has as a major objective the creation of block watch groups for the purpose of crime prevention. Originally, the staff member responsible for the project conducted door-to-door interviews to identify and coalesce residents in a one- or two-block area into a group which would then elect a block captain to serve as a contact person for the group. Often, because residents would not know each other or because they were not ready to organize, this process did not work. Now, key block members are identified in advance of a block meeting through word of mouth or by meeting active individuals in other neighborhood meetings. Nearly a dozen block groups have been convened in the first six months of the project, with the staff person serving as a consultant. Groups meet informally or maintain phone contact with each other. Although the groups are initially mobilized around the issue of crime, contact among neighbors becomes more generalized and some groups have assumed more "neighborly" roles. Often, contact with the block associations leads to identifying needy residents such as an isolated elderly person who may need other services from the agency's senior citizen program. This crosslinking is one example of the interweaving among program components and the helping networks they are fostering.

The community development component has been an active innovator in the neighborhood, bringing together a wide range of other types of networks, groups, and associations. An artists' union, now an informal network of individuals within the community, has been responsible for painting murals on buildings, and holding art fairs and educational programs for youth. One summer the union conducted a tour for children and youth called "Exploring Your Environment," in which groups of youth visited parts of the neighborhood to learn more about its history and develop an appreciation of the community's identity. A newer project of the community development component that is presently being developed through state funds is a self-help housing rehabilitation program. This program will create a skills bank in which local residents will have a clearinghouse for linking up with each other to trade skills in housing renovation and repair (e.g., wiring, plumbing,

TABLE 5.1   Combined Strategies with Strongest Impact on Generic
Outcome Criteria

Outcome Criteria	Combined Strategy
Accessibility	personal network, mutual aid and neighborhood helpers
Responsiveness	personal network and mutual aid
Client satisfaction and well being	mutual aid
Self-sufficiency	greater use of multiple approaches
Use of informal resources	greater use of multiple approaches
Deinstitutionalization	personal network and mutual aid
Efficiency	volunteer linking and mutual aid
Local control	greater use of multiple approaches

carpentry) as well as a tool bank from which local residents may
borrow tools to work on their houses.

[*Case No. 30*]

The Benefits of Combined Strategies

To assess the value of combining the five alternative strategies,
each program's assessed level of impact for particular outcome
criteria was compared with the overall number of different strategies
employed and with various combinations to determine the joint
effects of strategies. Table 5.1 lists the particular strategies or combinations of strategies that were most strongly associated with the
generic outcome criteria.

The findings in Table 5.1 show that in almost every instance, a
combination of strategies yielded the strongest impact on outcome
criteria. The exception was the mutual aid strategy which, when used
alone, made the strongest impact on the client's psychological and
emotional status. Agencies that used multiple strategies, whatever
the combination, attained the strongest impact in the areas of self-
sufficiency, use of informal resources, and local control. This may
reflect the fact that these agencies placed a greater emphasis on the
principles of self-reliance, self-help and participatory service delivery—in short, on involvement as an end in itself.

The joint use of the personal network and mutual aid strategies was most successful in improving agency responsiveness and reducing client institutionalization. The addition of the neighborhood helping strategy to this combination improved the accessibility and acceptability of services. This combination of three strategies relied on a wide range of informal helpers in reducing social isolation, meeting special needs, and promoting awareness of available services. Also, the helping activities in this combination of strategies were generally not specialized, involved little training or supervision of helpers, and depended mostly on the value of social support and interpersonal relationships for achieving objectives.

Finally, the joint use of the volunteer linking and mutual aid strategies made the strongest impact on the criterion of efficiency. By combining the use of trained and supervised lay helpers with the use of client involvement in mutual aid activities, clients with special needs such as the disabled could be served through less expensive means than if only paid staff were involved.

Discussion

Combining strategies offers more opportunities for different types of informal helpers to become involved. This serves a wider variety of purposes and provides greater flexibility for staff in addressing different problems. One program saw the strategies as a progressive series for integrating an individual within a community in which each strategy—from personal networking to community empowerment— offered increasing opportunities and demands for social participation. In this way, clients could progress from integration in a personal network to participation in helping others whether in a mutual aid network, a neighborhood, or the broader community.

Three major orientations are suggested by the combined strategies for working with informal helpers used by the agencies in our study. The orientation taken by some agencies emphasizes the involvement of informal resources in service delivery out of concern for client self-determination, a belief in self-help as a valued mode of problem-solving, and an emphasis on local participation in the design and delivery of program services. These agencies used a greater number of strategies because they included informal helpers and other community members in everything they did. The orientation of a second group of agencies emphasized the value of social support and individual integration into an enduring set of primary social ties. These agencies used strategies that focused on personal networks, networks of mutual aid among people with similar problems and concerns, and neighborhood networks. The third agency orientation emphasized the specialized use of helpers to deal with the problems of specific populations in ways that were most cost efficient. This was reflected in the joint use of volunteer linking and mutual aid strategies. Since these three orientations suggest different purposes for linking professional care with informal resources, they can be expected to achieve quite different outcomes.

Chapter 6

THE ORGANIZATIONAL CONTEXT: THE AGENCY AND THE COMMUNITY SERVICE SYSTEM

The nature of the organization in which work with informal helping networks is embedded can make a big difference in the choice of informal helping systems to work with, and in the character of the relationships that agency staff develop with informal helping systems. The organization of the broader community service system also affects programs which combine professional and informal sources of help. The general question of how informal helping fits into a human service agency becomes mirrored in the broader question of how such an agency may fit into the community service system.

This chapter looks at the organizational environment—both internal and external to an agency—to describe how work with informal helping networks will be influenced by the context in which it takes place. In the next chapter, we will extend our analysis of context to include the neighborhood and community environment. Our intent in this chapter will be to describe both by case examples and analytic comparisons how features of the organizational environment may determine the sorts of relationships that are developed between professionals and informal helpers. Based on the contrasting environments observed among the agencies we have studied, we discuss what modifications may be necessary in program organization in order to successfully work with informal helping networks.

The Agency

Agency attributes influence program outcomes because they help to determine the resources available to the program as well as the internal processes that impinge on the program. For example, a large agency may be more likely to have enough staff to develop several strategies using informal helpers and to combine these with more conventional direct service programs. However, a large agency may also be likely to rely on specialists and professionals, and to employ routinized approaches to service delivery and coordination which may reduce the ability of staff to respond to natural helpers in non-traditional, nonroutine ways.

The influence of an agency's organization can be examined by looking at the structure of the agency and the climate of work relationships among agency members. The structure of the agency will be reflected in the scale of operations, the degree of formalization and use of professional authority, and the stability of the agency. Work climate refers to the types of relationships among staff reflected in such factors as the style of leadership and the presence of peer support. We can understand the importance of structure and work climate by analyzing whether coordinative, collegial, or directive relationships developed between staff and informal helpers. The summary of this analysis is shown in Table 6.1. We will discuss each factor in turn.

AGENCY STRUCTURE

Human service agencies, as with most other organizations, strive to achieve control over their output—services—by relying on standard, formal rules for conducting tasks, making decisions, getting authorization, and assigning responsibility for tasks, clients, and so on. Although most agencies must have some such standards in order to conduct their business, there are wide variations both in the degree to which standards are relied on and in the severity of the sanctions imposed on staff for failure to follow standard procedures. This attribute of agency organization is termed formalization. Formalization simply means that the assignment of responsibilities (such as clients, tasks, and so on), the organization of the work flow, and the coordination of decision-making (that is, the "when," "where," "who," and "how" of the agency's work) are handled through standard, generally uniform, often written procedures (Hall, 1979).

TABLE 6.1   Agency Influences on Relationship

Organizational Structure	Coordinative	Collegial	Directive
Degree of Formalization	–	0	++
Use of Paraprofessional Staff	0	+	–
Size of Staff (FTE)	0	0	0
Size of Population Served	—	0	++
Stability of Agency Funding	–	0	++
Age of Agency	–	0	+
Work Climate			
Directive Style of Leadership	0	–	+
Supportive Style of Leadership	0	+	–
Level of Peer Support	++	+	–

Key: (–) or (—) refers to relative significance of negative correlation.
        (+) or (++) refers to significance of positive correlation.
        (0) reflects no significant relationship.

Some students of human service delivery systems have argued that in most instances it is dysfunctional for human service organizations to become highly formalized due to the limitations of the existing technology in human services for dealing with uncertainties and nonroutine situations (Litwak, 1978b; Sarri & Hasenfeld, 1978). As an alternative to trying to develop standardized rules and procedures to cover every contingency, an agency can rely on the abilities of the individual staff members to understand the agency's mission and to employ their own intuition, knowledge, and problem-solving skills to deal with the clients, problems, and situations that they encounter. Formalization is more appropriate in those organizations that deal with materials and technologies that are stable and certain.

When instituting new programs, as was the case for the agencies in this study, both the nature of the desired outcome and the technology for achieving that outcome are more untried, novel, and undeveloped than usual human service programming. Premature formalization of such a program may limit or constrain the program staff's ability to reach the program's objectives. The degree of agency formalization, then, may have a significant impact on program functioning.

We measured agency formalization by rating the degree to which the agency emphasized centralized management authority, formal procedures of staff supervision, professional standards of service, and professional credentials in staff selection. We found that a high degree of emphasis on these aspects of agency operation was significantly correlated with the development of a directive type of relationship between staff and helpers in which helpers were supervised, monitored, and given less responsibility for tasks. In contrast, the development of a coordinative or collegial type of relationship was related to less emphasis on formalization. These findings are augmented by the correlations between the three relationships and use of paraprofessional staff within agencies. Here, the development of a directive relationship with participants was negatively correlated with increasing agency use of paraprofessional staff in providing services.

These results suggest that agencies which give greater emphasis to bureaucratic procedures, professional norms, and formal authority in service delivery are less likely to develop participatory roles with the community that emphasize mutual decision-making and shared responsibility. Bureaucratization within an agency can lead to bureaucratization of the relationship with informal helping systems. To the extent that this is deemed an undesirable outcome, bureaucratized agencies will need to either adopt program strategies that are compatible with a more structured type of relationship or make adaptations in the structure to accommodate a program that differs from the agency norm.

The scale of an agency's operation also influenced the type of relationship adopted. Agency scale was examined by looking at the size of the community population served by the agency and the number of staff working with helpers. Agencies with larger population areas more often adopted a directive relationship with participants; those in smaller communities showed a tendency to adopt a coordinative relationship. One explanation for these findings would be that agencies with small population service areas (e.g., a neighborhood) were able to develop a greater familiarity with the community and then accord helpers greater responsibility. Agencies with larger areas (e.g., citywide) were likely to be more remote from the immediate environments within the community. Having less familiarity, they adopted a more directive stance with those they recruited.

Staff size as another indicator of agency scale did not correlate significantly with any of the types of staff-helper relationships.

The last aspect of agency structure we examined concerned the stability of the agency. Agency stability was measured both by continuity of funding and by how long the agency had been in operation. The two factors reflect the degree of certainty or consistency of agency operations and hence imply how changeable agency structure may be. The factor of agency stability reveals a rather surprising association with the type of relationships developed. Older agencies (i.e., longer number of years in operation) with more stable funding showed a tendency to adopt more directive relationships while younger agencies with uncertain funding from year to year were associated with more coordinative relationships. Agency stability was not related to the development of a collegial type of relationship. This may indicate that more mature agencies are less likely to risk the uncertainties of more equilateral participation, preferring to retain more authority by supervising and monitoring the work of participants. Older and more stable agencies may also have become specialized and routinized in their methods of operation with procedures instituted that offered a more restricted range of opportunities for participation. The cross-sectional nature of our study did not permit such an explanation to be examined here, although studies of organizational growth suggest that the explanation is plausible (see Downs, 1967).

WORK CLIMATE

While structural attributes influence program functioning, the interpersonal processes and relationships among personnel and staff within the organization will also have a major impact. Interpersonal orientations, attachments, conflicts, and attitudes can shape the manner in which the agency functions, as well as how tasks and responsibilities are perceived and performed by staff. These processes create the "work climate," which some researchers have found can influence the ability of an organization to implement changes or adopt innovations (Michael, 1973; Zaltman, Duncan & Holbek, 1973). These interpersonal processes can be grouped into two main types of relations, those between superior and subordinate persons with different levels of authority and responsibility within the organization (leadership factors), and those between co-workers or colleagues (peer factors).

Organizations differ in the way that leadership roles are assigned. In some instances, the leadership positions are assigned to persons based on an assessment of their superior skills, competence, or experience. In others, factors of interpersonal skill and personality or charisma are given more weight. Task leadership is based primarily on technical competence and is a precursor to a directive leadership style. Expressive leadership is based primarily on interpersonal competence and leads to a supportive leadership style (Etzioni, 1975; Hall, 1979). The two types of leaders have different patterns of communication with their subordinates: The task leader tends to emphasize instructions and decisions that come from managers and administrators regarding specific work tasks and techniques, while the expressive leader provides positive feedback on work performance, gives information and advice, and listens to the opinions and frustrations of the subordinates. No organization is likely to rely solely on either type of leadership, but there is a tendency for organizations to emphasize one leadership style over the other.

For example, in one program serving the elderly, the program manager generally used a directive leadership approach. She held regular staff meetings to inform staff of her decisions, to instruct them as to changes in tasks and assignments, and to check on their performance with the supervisors present. She asked that all problems with clients or work assignments be taken up with the immediate supervisor and/or with herself, rather than with other co-workers. In a contrasting situation in another small program for the elderly, the program manager used a supportive leadership style. She channeled information to staff as needed, worked with them individually on problems as they occurred, and praised them for work well done. In the first program the manager was respected, but avoided and perhaps feared by her subordinate staff, while in the second program the manager was also respected but her staff were more likely to seek her out for advice, information, and assistance in improving skills and performance. The two leadership styles thus involve different degrees of autonomy and trust given to staff by the program manager.

Among the agencies in our study, the directive leadership style was correlated with the directive relationship style and the supportive leadership style with the collegial relationship style. This finding suggests that the program manager plays a critical role in shaping the staff relationships with informal helpers. The leadership style of the manager can mediate the structure of the agency. Thus, a highly bureaucratized agency could select a program manager that had a supportive leadership style if a collegial type of relationship between staff and informal helper was considered more appropriate for the tasks at hand.

Peer support among staff also exerts an important mediating influence on agency structure in the development of relationships between staff and helper. Research and experience suggest that positive interpersonal relationships among co-workers involving sharing information, advice, encouragement, standing in for each other, and an atmosphere in which giving and asking for help are supported lead to employee job satisfaction and high morale (Armstrong, 1977). Such positive, supportive exchanges are particularly important in situations where an agency is undertaking a program innovation. This type of situation may require basic changes in the types of knowledge and tasks that staff are expected to employ, in goals and values for the organization, or in the way in which the organization exchanges information with other agencies in its environment (Zaltman et al., 1973). In such novel, nonroutine situations where the uncertainty about technology and methods is high, staff must usually place greater reliance on each other and on their interpersonal communication, risk-taking, and problem-solving skills.

In general, low peer support among staff was more characteristic of agencies that developed a directive relationship with informal helpers, while those that developed coordinative relationships more typically displayed high peer support. For example, a program which reflected low peer support among staff and had developed directive relationships with informal helpers had only one half-time and one quarter-time staff position. Here, each staff person had separate roles and responsibilities and a very limited amount of time in which to accomplish fairly ambitious objectives. The two staff members engaged in very little interpersonal communication and only infrequently exchanged ideas and advice. Although a highly placed agency administrator was supportive of the program and of the individual staff members, other intervening midlevel managers and agency staff (mostly clinically oriented) had little understanding or commitment to the informal helper program.

The agencies that had developed coordinative relationships with helpers had programs that were small, with only two or three staff members. Staff in these programs often worked very closely with each other, although each could also have independent responsibilities. For example, in one program serving an inner city, ethnic, working-class neighborhood, the staff consisted of two full time persons. These staff worked with a number of self-help and planning groups (volunteers), and with an agency steering committee with the goal of improving services and strengthening informal supports within this neighborhood. The staff closely coordinated their efforts and also had backup support from research staff in the sponsoring body, as well as from a local professional advisory group.

An effective work climate encourages information-sharing and problem-solving and reduces stress and anxiety among agency staff, thereby enhancing agency functioning. Agency staff often experienced the need to overcome their sense of uncertainty and isolation. This need was usually met by encouraging staff to share problems, ideas, and information with each other, to have joint problem-solving sessions. In this way each person could draw not only on their personal repertoire of technical skills and life experiences, but on the skills, insights, and understandings of other staff. Even small programs capitalized on this staff need for information-sharing and stress-reduction by using part-time staff or an occasional outside consultant, or by linking up with larger agencies for professional as well as administrative support.

Overall, our findings regarding both agency structure and work climate show how important the organizational context internal to an agency can be in work with informal helping networks. Agency structure influences the availability of staff, needs for coordination, the demands on management, and nature of leadership. In turn, these factors influence the degree of flexibility the agency will have in being able to adopt new and untried service programs. These sets of factors provide a background for the agency's work environment, which heavily influences the support, autonomy, and feedback available to staff. Work environment, and particularly the availability of staff support, also exert a major influence on the nature of the relationship that will be developed with informal helpers.

The Community Service System

It would be a mistake to assume that the decision-making and performance of an organization could be fully understood by examining only those factors that are inherent to the agency. Human service or social welfare organizations are particularly susceptible to influence from the environment due to the permeability of their boundaries (Smith, 1970), and to their dependency on external collectivities for the allocation of resources and for validation and acceptance of their services (Sarri & Hasenfeld, 1978). For most human service agencies, the relevant environment is the set of external organizations and groups which the agency relies on for its day-to-day activities—funding and regulatory bodies, and social service agencies and other institutions in the same community, particularly those serving the same population.

Most of the agencies in our study were quite tightly linked into other human service agencies in their communities. In many cases, this was an outgrowth of an agency's affiliation or departmental tie to a larger agency. Most agencies were funded by several sources and therefore were required to keep in active communication with several agencies. Thus, the most typical relationship of the agency with other services in a community was one of active exchange and mutual interdependence. The potential for competition and various forms of indirect influence was more difficult to assess, but at least some estimates of these effects can be made.

An agency's relationship with the community service system is fairly complex and elusive, and consequently we will rely extensively on case examples from our study to illustrate possibilities. The relationship is also not a one-way proposition: The agency influences the larger system just as it is influenced in turn. To suggest the range of exchanges, we looked at four major areas of interaction: case referral and client advocacy, interagency coordination, interagency competition, and indirect types of interaction. Our overall interest will be to outline the broader implications of the agency's efforts for the environment in which it must operate.

CASE REFERRAL AND CLIENT ADVOCACY

Most of the programs were involved in a two-way flow of client referrals for specific services. Several programs were heavily dependent on referrals from other agencies for clients. In some cases this worked well, while in other cases this limitation caused difficulties. The contrasting experience of two agencies in our study, both of which served families with young children, illustrates the possible dynamics of referral relationships. Both agencies depended heavily on doctors and other hospital personnel to tell parents of newborns about their programs. One agency which offered informal discussion groups for young mothers had excellent cooperation from hospital staff. The nursing staff routinely handed out their brochures to all new mothers. In contrast, the other agency offered peer support to parents of retarded children and found it much more difficult to secure referrals. Agency staff felt that hospital personnel needed to meet them and the parent volunteers face-to-face on a frequent basis in order to maintain the necessary level of confidence in the service being offered and to remember to suggest it to new parents when a retarded child was born. Therefore a significant amount of staff and volunteer time had to be spent contacting and recontacting referral sources.

Two factors may account for the difference between the referral experiences of the two agencies. The agency which provided support groups for young mothers offered a low-key, nonthreatening service which built upon the generally positive experience of having a new baby. The other agency wished to help parents who were in a crisis situation and might be perceived by professionals as especially vulnerable and in need of some protection and careful handling. The birth of retarded children is also a less common event and the hospital staff is less likely to remember to suggest the agency since the occasion arises less often.

That neither of these problems is insurmountable is shown by another agency that provides lay therapists to child abusing families. In some ways this agency's situation is similar to that of the agency providing services to parents of the retarded. The agency also provides a service to families in crisis and deals with a problem that occurs relatively infrequently in the general population; yet it has no difficulty getting referrals from other formal agencies. This success in obtaining referrals may stem from a relatively longer period of operation in which the confidence of formal service providers in the agency's service has grown over time. Thus, agencies which deal with more threatening or less common problems may have to work harder to get referrals. This type of agency may also have to allow more time for relationships to develop with other agencies in the community. Agencies which are more preventively focused and deal with a general population will probably have less difficulty in gaining acceptance.

Another sort of referral problem was experienced by an agency which provided personal advocacy services for adult mentally retarded persons living in the community. The agency needed to obtain referrals from other programs serving this group, such as sheltered workshops and group homes, since it had no way of reaching the group directly. However, advocacy on behalf of a client occasionally put the agency in a position antagonistic to that of one of these other services. In order to prevent these instances from causing general suspicion and mistrust, the agency had to work hard to keep lines of communication open to other service agencies and to cooperate with them whenever possible.

When the staff in the agencies in our sample made referrals to other agencies they emphasized a "personal touch." Staff tended to refer to specific individuals at another agency with whom they had a relationship, rather than making a more general referral. They often stayed involved with the client or helper, bringing the professional worker from another agency to the client's home or taking the client in for an appointment to be sure that the appropriate service was delivered. Finally, they made a point of checking back with the client (and sometimes with the agency) to see whether any further action was necessary. Agency staff in our sample may have been more careful than many workers are in their referrals because they were concerned about maintaining their credibility with the neighborhood or target group they were serving. If the referral went badly and the client was not satisfied with the service they received, the staff would be likely to hear about it because of their accessibility and multiple sources of information. Others in the neighborhood or group would hear about it also and this would have damaging repercussions, not only for the further use of that service but for the general reputation of the agency staff person who had made the referral.

In another type of active client-centered exchange, we found a number of instances where agency staff or informal helpers acted as advocates with other staff members of their own agencies and with other agencies serving the same clientele. Sometimes this occurred primarily on an individual basis. For example, a staff member or helper might accompany a non-English speaking person to an appointment at the welfare office or get a lawyer for a retarded adult who wanted to move out of a group home against parental wishes. At other times, the advocacy took the form of persuading various community agencies to station personnel in an area they had previously not been serving or to develop a new service tailored to the needs and cultural style of the area. Often, the staff of agencies in our study were seen as "experts" on the neighborhood or client group by workers in other agencies and were asked by the agencies to perform various bridging functions. While a certain amount of this was seen as unavoidable, the goal of most agencies was to move out of the role of middleman and to facilitate the direct involvement of other agencies with clients or informal helpers.

INTERAGENCY COORDINATION

Most human service agencies engage in activities with other agencies in the community to establish some degree of coordination in each organization's procedures and services. For agencies in our study, these activities generally involved participating in joint planning activities with existing programs or discussing the development of new programs. However, the level of their involvement with other agencies in planning councils or other ad hoc joint planning activities varied widely. Some agencies helped to develop such councils as a program objective and engaged in extensive planning with other agencies before initiating their programs. Other agencies were invited to join planning councils after establishing their "credibility" through their service program.

There were some programs which did not develop much interaction with other agencies. In some cases, being closely identified with the target population, especially if it was an underserved or minority one, created antagonisms with other agencies which made closer contact difficult even though it was desired by the agency. In other cases, the agency deliberately avoided closer contact because it was seen as detrimental to the establishment of rapport with the target group. For example, one program on an Indian reservation was very careful to choose which agencies to become associated with in joint planning activities because the more traditional Indians to whom they hoped to appeal were very distrustful of some of the agencies on the reservation which they perceived as being dominated by white values and policies.

Another program for the elderly referred clients to various social services when appropriate but was careful to avoid too close an integration of services that might result from allowing their facilities to be used or participating on planning councils. They felt that their clientele of elderly persons living in their own homes were generally opposed to "welfare" or "mental health" as well as to forms of advocacy like the Gray Panthers and therefore would not use the center if it were associated with these services or organizations.

INTERAGENCY COMPETITION

Thomas (1979) has suggested that, as the interest in linking formal services more closely to informal caregiving grows, there will be more instances of dysfunctional competition. Interagency competition for access to informal sources of care is one form this competition could take.

Rivalry among agencies for informal helpers may occur as more agencies come to see such local figures as hairdressers, shopkeepers, and helping neighbors as resources. As a consequence, agency staff may come to make multiple demands on them. This possibility becomes more likely when programs are based on categories of need, since most informal helpers offer assistance to people they know in a way which ignores such categorical distinctions. Consequently a community mental health center, a senior center, and a youth agency might all identify the same waitress in a coffee shop as important to their various clienteles. Agencies which utilize volunteers to perform fairly time-consuming or difficult tasks (befriending a retarded adult who is trying to live independently in the community, or serving as a companion to a parent in a violence prone family) may find that the pool of volunteers in any community with the time and talents for such efforts is very limited. Informal resources can be just as scarce as professional resources. The agencies in our study did not encounter a great deal of competition for helpers primarily because there were not enough other agencies interested in relating to informal helpers to exhaust available resources. This could be an increasingly important problem in the future, however. Competition among agencies for informal helpers could also have deleterious effects on the morale of the helpers and increase community members' mistrust of formal services.

INDIRECT INFLUENCES

Aside from the direct forms of interaction among agencies involving coordination or competition, there were a number of other less direct ways in which an agency's work with informal helpers could influence other agencies in the community. Sometimes these indirect influences were relatively clearly observed. For example, many of the agencies in our study could point to "graduates" of their programs who had become staff or board members of other agencies. Participation in these programs was just part of their ongoing involvement in the community. This was particularly true of neighborhood and role-related helpers. Others who were involved initially as volunteers, members of mutual aid groups, or recipients of services developed a wider outlook as they were treated by agency staff as peers who had a general interest in the goals of the agency. These people carried the philosophy of the program into new positions of community leadership.

In other instances, the indirect influence of an agency's work with informal helpers on community services might be less clearly seen. Many of the programs in our study could have an effect on the demand for other services in the community because of the impact of their efforts on behalf of a target population. For example, several programs could demonstrate a reduction in the use of institutional services for their clients. Reduced hospital stays, fewer entries into nursing homes, and reduced use of outpatient care have all been shown to be consequences of the efforts of a number of agencies in our study. Clearly, if the efforts of such agencies could be multiplied so as to achieve a much larger scale of impact, the types and amounts of services needed in a community could be substantially altered.

Alternatively, in a number of other agencies, staff efforts were directed to essentially increasing the demand for other community services. One way this was accomplished was through the attention given to casefinding by agency staff. For example, an explicit purpose of an agency that served parents of developmentally disabled children was to inform them of appropriate and available services. Many other programs did not have casefinding as an explicit objective, but they were often the first agency to become aware of an individual with many needs because of their general visibility and accessibility in the community.

Demands for community services could have also been increased through the advocacy efforts of a number of agencies we studied. For example, several agencies which were dealing with the physically and mentally disabled encouraged and supported the efforts of clients and informal helpers to assert their rights and get needed services for themselves. They also trained volunteers to become advocates for such persons. Another program helped to form constituent groups among various service clientele. These groups then became a new force in the community and participated in planning for services. In another instance, an agency established a program that was originally intended to provide individual and group support to people caring for elderly relatives. In addition to performing this function, staff found that the caregivers identified policy issues regarding the eligibility of their elderly relatives for various services and the general availability and quality of home-based services. The program helped these groups articulate these concerns to state and federal legislative bodies.

Conclusion

This chapter has discussed how the overall organizational context plays a significant role in the way an agency's staff will work with informal helping networks. We have looked at the organizational context as a matter of the structure and climate of the agency as well as in respect to the interagency interactions occurring with the broader community service system.

For those who would like to adopt an informal helper program, it is necessary to assess what aspects of the agency's structure or work climate are amenable to control or regulation and which aspects are givens, i.e., are not likely to be allowed to vary or change in the agency. The program planner should also be aware that agency context can have an impact on which types of interactions or relationships with informal helpers are most amenable to adoption. Program strategies may be adapted to almost any agency context, but the process of adaptation will work best when attention is given to such factors as the placement of the program within the agency, the selection of the program manager, and the nature of the task assignment for individual staff members, as well as to more conventional considerations regarding the desired outcomes for clients. There is no simple pattern of association that can be described between agency context and program functioning.

Our analysis of the interaction between an agency and the system of other agencies serving the community indicates a number of areas where an attempt to link professional and informal helpers will be both influenced and influential. Informal helpers can make a substantial impact on the system by performing such roles as advocates, casefinders, resource brokers, and monitors. In other instances, the community service system may exert its own influence on the efforts of staff and informal helpers. In some cases this may be a facilitating influence as referral avenues are kept open and efficient. The system can also be a hindrance, as when competition for resources is detrimental to staff working with informal helpers or when the general reputation of the service system is so negative that informal helpers do not want to be involved with the agency.

Chapter 7

THE NEIGHBORHOOD AS A CONTEXT AND RESOURCE FOR HELPING

The social networks which form the basis for informal helping vary in structure and content from community to community as well as from individual to individual. At the neighborhood level, there are variations in the strength of the ties between members of one community compared to another, in the density of the interconnections, and in the types of organizations within which ties are formed and maintained. Each of these variations has an impact on the approaches that formal agencies can use to work with the informal helping system within a specific community or neighborhood.

The intent of this chapter is to draw from the experience of the agencies in our study to provide suggestions and observations about program strategies which are successful in neighborhoods or communities with different characteristics. Not all of the agencies we observed were focusing on neighborhoods. Some programs were not locality-based because the immediate locality was not relevant for their target populations. Most often these agencies addressed populations that represented a small and widely-scattered minority in the area; for example, none of the programs for the developmentally or physically disabled focused on a neighborhood. The local area may also be inappropriate as a source of informal help when the focal problem is stigmatizing and the clients wish to remain anonymous, e.g., child abuse, battering of women, or mental problems. A neighborhood-based approach is most appropriate when the target problem concerns a large subgroup of the population such as the elderly; when clients may be spatially clustered, such as former mental patients; or when the focus is on prevention of problems. Focusing on prevention allows the agency to work with the larger group of the population at risk, for example, new parents or people with life crisis, rather than with the smaller groups of child abusers or mental patients.

The discussion in this chapter concentrates on those agencies for which the neighborhood was important to the delivery of services; that is, those where staff activities were differentiated by neighborhood, or where the staff were aware of the influence of neighborhood characteristics on the delivery of services. A total of nineteen programs were defined as locality-based. Five of the agencies were implementing programs in more than one neighborhood, allowing comparisons of how neighborhoods influenced the implementation and success of the program.

The Relevance of Neighborhood

At the outset it will be useful to briefly clarify what we mean in referring to the "neighborhood" both as a concept and a setting for informal helping. The concept of "neighborhood" is defined in a variety of ways depending on which of the functions of the neighborhood is emphasized. For example, the neighborhood as defined by the area in which neighbors know each other and exchange minor favors is generally quite small—a block or so. In some areas no such exchanges take place. On the other hand, the neighborhood with which one identifies in response to the question "where do you live" or which has a generally agreed upon name or forms the basis for political action is usually a larger area, perhaps a square mile in size. Depending on density, the population of such an area can vary widely.

It is with neighborhoods defined in this larger sense that locality-based programs chose to work. The size of the neighborhoods in our study ranged from under 100 residents (a community on a Sioux reservation) to over 100,000 residents (several sections of New York City). While the latter are obviously larger than the area typically labeled a neighborhood, they allow comparison of the effectiveness of an approach in areas which differ widely in their demographic characteristics. Overall, about one-third of the locality-based programs worked in neighborhoods with populations between five and ten thousand, and an additional one-third in neighborhoods with populations between ten and fifty thousand. Six of the programs were in rural areas or small towns.

Much of the sociological analysis of urban life since Durkheim (1933) and Wirth (1938) has argued that the neighborhood is an unlikely base for informal social exchange in an urban and urbanized society such as ours. Wirth, for example, argued that social relationships in urban areas are transitory, nonintimate, and governed by the limited role relationships in which they occur, such as customer-clerk or fellow worker. However, other social scientists studying neighborhoods within urban settings have rediscovered communities based on close, primary ties (Gans, 1962; Stack, 1974; Young & Willmott, 1957). Such areas often function as "urban villages" held together by proximity and ethnicity or social class. These two visions of the urban neighborhood serve as extreme opposite ends of a continuum of neighborhood types and personal lifestyles. Most individuals are enmeshed in a network of social relationships which includes personal and intimate relations as well as the secondary and segmental relations identified by Wirth and others. Thus, while the individual's strongest and most intimate ties are often no longer bound by locality (Webber, 1963; Wellman, 1979), the neighbor role remains. Many people rely on their neighbors for aid in emergencies and everyday exchanges (Litwak & Szelenyi, 1969), even if they do not count their neighbors among their intimates. Keller (1968) observed that there is a neighboring role which is not identical to the role of the friend, and which typically includes informal helping as one of the expectations of being a "good neighbor."

Reliance on the neighborhood as a source of help is most likely to occur in situations requiring short-term or emergency aid, such as looking after a child for an hour or taking someone to the hospital, rather than in situations requiring long-term help such as caring for someone recuperating from an operation (Litwak & Szelenyi, 1969). Certain sectors of the population are probably more likely than others to rely on the neighborhood as a source of social contact and exchange, particularly those who are limited in their mobility out of the neighborhood—children and their nonworking mothers, the elderly, and the unemployed. Thus, while neighborhoods are not the focus of the most intimate social relations for most people, they may act as such for some subgroups of the population. In addition, they have the potential to serve as the locality for informal helping on the small scale and political action on the larger scale.

The Impact of Neighborhood or Community Characteristics

We anticipated that characteristics of the neighborhood or community would have a strong influence on the best approach to working with that community. Such characteristics as the economic, demographic, and subcultural characteristics of the population were expected to have an effect on the structure of the informal helping network and the norms that governed its functioning. The structure and functions of the informal network in turn have implications for the agency's choice of strategies for working with that network. We found the four most influential characteristics to be the homogeneity of the neighborhood, cultural traditions, the stability of the neighborhood, and the institutions or behavior settings that knit the community together.

HETEROGENEITY

Perceived differences among the residents of a community can be based on a variety of factors such as race or ethnicity, social status, life cycle stage, or kinship. To the extent there is a diverse or heterogeneous population, there may be barriers to the development of informal helping across those lines. Thus, heterogeneity can be a hindering factor in developing a successful program. This is not to say that programs directed to a homogeneous community will not face difficulties. While homogeneous communities may have more active informal systems, they are also at times harder for outsiders such as agency staff to enter.

Differences in race or ethnicity can act as a barrier particularly when there are recent and rapid changes in the ethnic make-up of an area, or when ethnic differences are also associated with status differences. Two communities in Philadelphia and Chicago had experienced a very rapid change from white to black residents, accompanied by "block-busting" tactics from some of the local realtors. In both instances differences in life cycle stage between old and new residents also resulted as older whites remained behind and young black families moved in. Agency staff found it difficult to generate any informal helping exchange due to the age differences and to feelings of fear and threat engendered by racial differences and the block-busting tactics. Yet, in an adjacent neighborhood in Philadelphia that had become racially integrated more gradually and had a more balanced age mix, the agency was able to generate such exchanges. Paying black youth to visit and help elderly white neighbors was one approach that succeeded in overcoming interracial fear on an individual basis.

Ethnic differences are often compounded by status differences among residents. A program in Texas which organized task forces of the elderly to help other elderly neighbors within an Hispanic neighborhood found that informal helpers were often reluctant to extend their help to the Anglo sector of the neighborhood. This reluctance stemmed not only from ethnic differences but also from status differences—the Hispanics failed to see how the presumably more affluent Anglos could need their help. On the other hand, a program in rural Arizona found that the Anglos and Hispanics with similar social status generally worked well together, but that little help was offered to the Papago Indians in the same community despite their obvious need. These examples support Gans's (1961) argument that social status homogeneity is more important than racial homogeneity in working with neighborhood residents, at least when racial differences are not associated with rapid changes in a neighborhood.

Age and social status differences can be divisive factors in neighborhoods independent of racial characteristics. In one program, elderly homeowners were reluctant to welcome residents of SRO hotels into activities in the senior center. Similarly, another agency which was forming a club for seniors in a neighborhood found that over time one group, the middle-class homeowners, became predominant while the others, residents of high-rise apartments and board-and-care homes, dropped out or were excluded.

Finally, differences between agency staff and neighborhood residents on these characteristics are as crucial to the ability of the agency to support informal helping as are differences within the community. For example, agencies working with black or Hispanic populations found it helpful, and in some cases essential, to employ staff with the same ethnic identity in order to gain entry into the community, communicate with the residents, and establish mutual trust. Social class differences also can be barriers. An agency with a program for mothers of newborn infants aimed at preventing child abuse found that the model they had developed based on their middle-class experience worked well in a middle-class neighborhood but was much less successful in a working-class neighborhood where certain values regarding childrearing were not prevalent (e.g., the importance of reading books, talking to experts, and sharing problems). The working-class mothers were also not comfortable meeting in their homes or assuming group leadership.

CULTURAL TRADITIONS

The shared cultural traditions within a neighborhood or community can either facilitate or hinder the informal helping process. For example, staff in many of the locality-based agencies found that norms of self-reliance barred developing mutual aid. Self-reliance often translated into a suspicion of formal agencies and a view of formal services as unwanted "charity," rather than an emphasis on individualism. This underlying concern might best be defined as one of self-determination, of maintaining control over what happens, and of having choices. Program staff who enter a community with few set notions about specific solutions to problems or community needs are likely to encounter less resistance than those who enter with a specific model and are unable to change it to fit the community's perception of needs and appropriate solutions. While the latter were most likely to report that the community was very self-reliant, this may have been simply the way the community expressed resistance or indifference to the agency's program.

Cultural traditions in a community often involve unwritten rules about who should exchange help and what kind of help is appropriate within the informal network as well as from professionals. Staff who are part of a program to develop specific helping skills based on counseling techniques in rural communities in Pennsylvania found that the local norms against sharing feelings and toward self-reliance in general made it difficult to develop community support for the goals and methods of the program.

In other cases, cultural traditions that stress the importance of the family may prevent the development of a sense of community and hinder neighborhood helping activities. In one Hispanic community, for example, many families were insulted by offers of help from outsiders. In this case it proved possible to draw on shared religious traditions to extend helping from the family to the community. Another program on an Indian reservation was less successful in developing a sense of community and mutual aid that crossed family lines. The system of interfamily conflict proved so strong that it could not be overcome at the community level by appealing to the restoration of traditional values.

POPULATION STABILITY

Neighborhood stability was considered a factor that aided program success by the staff of a number of neighborhood agencies. Stability appears to be most relevant to programs which are attempting to foster ongoing informal helping arrangements that occur spontaneously, outside the confines of organized contact such as a mutual aid group. While stability need not imply that there is an active network of social interaction, it does usually imply a base of acquaintance upon which a more active network can be built.

Unstable communities will have different potential for developing informal helping depending on the specific reasons which account for the instability. For example, communities that are in the process of changing from one population to another are quite different from those that have a transient population, such as students or young singles. As discussed earlier, it proved very difficult to encourage informal helping across group lines when a rapid change in population had occurred. On the other hand, informal helping was successfully initiated within the group moving into the area.

Rural communities undergoing "suburbanization" present another set of problems in which two factions—inmigrants and natives—may have conflicting sets of values. A rural community in Massachusetts that had a new housing development serving universities in nearby towns experienced increasing conflict between the old residents with historical roots in the town whose lives centered around farming, the extended family, and traditional values, and the new residents with more professional, mobile, and modern values. While informal helping was active among the older residents, their distrust of outsiders and formal services, exacerbated by their feeling that the newcomers posed a threat, made it difficult for the representatives of the formal agency to develop a legitimate supporting role in the community.

Instability may be hardest to overcome when a neighborhood is composed of short-term transitory groups who have relatively little identification with the neighborhood. Despite this caveat, several programs were able to involve a transient population of students in more structured informal helping roles such as volunteers or as participants in groups that maintained an identity although individual members came and went. Another kind of transitory group is the population which has developed a cyclical pattern of movements, for example, between the Indian reservation and the city, or between the United States and Puerto Rico. Agencies found it difficult to rely on natural helpers in these communities since they were apt to be part of this recurring cycle of migration.

INTEGRATING INSTITUTIONS

Active informal helping networks within a neighborhood may also be partially due to the presence of places or institutions which allow and encourage people from the locality to get together in the course of their daily lives. The concept of the "behavior setting" can be used to refer to places where particular types of activities tend to occur (Barker, 1978). Behavior settings that might encourage neighboring acquaintance and exchange could include a grocery store that serves a small clientele and provides chairs or a snack bar where people might linger, a community baseball game, or a meeting of a senior's group in one of the churches. The activities may be very much influenced by the social norms and physical environment of that setting: whether there are high fences, people walk regularly, or there are neighborhood stores and churches. Settings of relevance to informal helping can range from formal, organized settings and institutions to less organized and more spontaneous social encounters.

Institutions such as schools, religious institutions, neighborhood organizations, and businesses which serve a limited local area can be very influential in uniting people within a neighborhood. Such institutions and behavior settings also were found to serve a variety of functions for clients of the agencies we studied. They were often the locus of natural helpers or of role-related helpers identified by the agency as helpers to their clients (see Chapter 2). These helpers were likely to contact many clients or potential clients because of their role in the setting: religious figure, storekeeper, postmistress, librarian.

In other cases, the institutions or behavior settings served as gathering places in which links could form among neighborhood residents. In many communities there were bars or cafes frequented by local residents. In one neighborhood in New York City some of these had developed into social clubs for the Puerto Rican residents. Each club served as a gathering place for people from a specific town or locality in Puerto Rico and sponsored social events. While these social events served to build social bonds among those who lived in the New York neighborhood, they also kept alive locality-based ties among people who were more than 1000 miles from the locale in which the ties had originated.

The opportunities for social contact are often more organized. In addition to religious institutions, organizations such as the volunteer fire department and its associated ladies auxiliary may serve as the center of social life in a rural area. They tend to gain in importance as other integrating institutions, such as school districts, become regionalized and lose their integrative function. In small towns, voluntary associations such as the Grange, Moose lodges, Masons, and labor unions often are important. These organizations are likely to be sources of ties to key people inside and outside the neighborhood who have the information and knowledge needed to solve personal and neighborhood problems (Warren & Warren, 1977).

Two examples from our study suggest how behavior settings can also play an important role in the work of programs for the former mental patient. A program in New York State for deinstitutionalized adults, both mental patients and the developmentally disabled, had established a comprehensive housing and training program to ease the transition of clients back into the community. Agency staff developed an array of means to integrate clients into the community, ranging from encouraging them to take part in free or inexpensive events in the community—the library, films on the college campus—to developing opportunities for more active involvement and even creating settings that involved their clients with others in the neighborhood, e.g., baseball games, dances.

This program also illustrates how a local cafe can serve as an integrating force for clients. A diverse group of individuals from the community surrounding a university organized the cafe on a completely voluntary, nonprofit basis to provide a place where neighborhood residents could meet to talk and have low cost nutritious meals. Agency staff who frequented the cafe discovered that mental patients who went there were treated very sensitively. In conjunction with community members, staff decided to enhance the function the cafe was already serving informally. A staff member from the agency volunteered to cook dinner one night a week with a group of the agency's present and former clients. Although more clients probably come to the cafe that night than usual, at least half of the patrons are regulars of the cafe. The cafe is a very valuable resource to the program and the neighborhood; the people who volunteer there tend to be excellent sources of information about services and ways to get things done.

The role of agency staff can vary from attempting to create behavior settings that bring the neighbors together, such as a neighborhood organization or a drop-in day care center, to integrating new people into existing settings, to creating new roles that encourage neighbor interaction. For example, block workers who are asked to deliver calendars to their neighbors listing monthly events at the senior center also have an excuse to stop and chat with their neighbors once a month. Without such agency-initiated opportunities to interact, neighbors may live side-by-side for years without developing relationships that allow them to exchange help when the need arises, or even to discover that there is a need.

Strategies for Different Types of Neighborhoods

The presence of neighborhood stability, certain cultural traditions, heterogeneity of population groups, and key integrating institutions or settings can influence the nature of the informal system of helping and the kind of role the agency can play in a community. These factors are important because they shape the amount and kind of social interaction among residents, influence residents' perception of a shared neighborhood identity, and influence the social, political, or economic linkages residents have to the broader community within which the neighborhood is situated. Warren and Warren (1977) have classified neighborhoods according to these three dimensions—social interaction, neighborhood identity, and external linkages with the community—and pointed out the extent to which the resulting types require different strategies for working with residents. We used their typology to classify the neighborhoods in our study. Several neighborhood types with which agency staff were working illustrate how strategies may be modified. It should be noted, however, that most of the neighborhood-oriented agencies we studied were working with neighborhoods wherein there was a high degree of social interaction among residents.

In one type of neighborhood, called parochial in the Warrens' typology, most residents know each other, interact often, and share a sense of neighborhood identity, but have few ties with the broader community and generally screen out what does not conform to their own norms. Staff working with parochial neighborhoods emphasized the very informal and personal elements of the network—neighbors and natural helpers. Since parochial neighborhoods tend to be well integrated internally and relatively isolated from the rest of the community, it was easier to work with the neighborhood as a system and less necessary to rely on the personal network of a particular client. Indeed, several agencies commented that parochial neighborhoods had traditionally relied heavily on informal and local sources of support, with a religious institution often playing an important role. Reliance on the informal system appeared to derive in part from constrained choices in lower income and minority areas and in part from normative preferences for nonpublic care (Abrams, 1978).

The experiences of several agencies suggest that natural helpers are not present in all communities, or that if they are present, staff find it difficult or impossible to identify them. In the case of one transitory community characterized by low social interaction and little neighborhood identity, program staff could not find people even in such central positions as ministers and school principals who could identify natural helpers. The more organized and less spontaneous helper roles—role-related helpers and people with similar problems—could be found and relied upon across neighborhoods that differed in their level of interaction, identity and ties with the broader community.

One agency working with three rural communities classified as transitory, parochial, and integral illustrates the necessity for different approaches with different types of neighborhoods. In the parochial community, the agency found that a strategy in which staff kept a low profile and relied heavily on the informal system of natural helpers was most effective. In an integral community characterized by high levels of neighborhood identity, interaction, and ties to the large society, it proved possible to work both with the informal system of helpers and with the formal system of governmental and other community leaders. The transitory community, however, was in a state of change that involved a clear conflict of values between the "oldtimers" and the "newcomers." The community of older residents was very suspicious of outsiders and the program staff had to move slowly, work with very concrete problems, and concentrate on working with the formal leadership of the town.

Another program working in a rural area found a similar problem of resistance to the program in one very rural, parochial area compared to greater success in an integral small town. This program involved a relatively formal training process for informal helpers and made extensive use of leaders of the formal system—government, religious institutions, local agencies—as entry points into the community. This strategy proved better suited to the functioning of the integral community with its vertical linkages than to the parochial community. A more informal approach through the community natural helpers might have been more successful in the parochial community.

Summary

This chapter has discussed the experiences of agencies which chose to focus on limited localities in working with informal helping networks. For those populations and problems for which it is suitable, a locality-based approach has a number of advantages. First, it allows the agency to deal with the area as an ecological system and to understand the functioning of an entire informal social network within a locality, rather than focusing on individuals simply as clients. It becomes practical at the neighborhood level to work with a whole community of different kinds of informal helpers and helping in order to meet the needs of clients.

A locality-based approach also allows an agency to work concurrently with more than one target population and at times to effectively combine programs. Such programs are more able to work with multiproblem families, for they have the potential to address a wide variety of problems and to take advantage of the numerous ties the family may or could have with the community. There is less need to coordinate through multiple programs on a citywide scale in order to handle such complex sets of problems. Programs which include more than one target population may also be able to make better use of natural helpers, since such helpers are often central to people whom agencies would classify as belonging to different target populations.

Finally, locality-based approaches can take advantage of some of the unique assets of neighbors as helpers: their ability to recognize a crisis and respond quickly, and the ease with which mutual aid can be integrated into everyday activities.

Chapter 8

MODIFYING THE PROFESSIONAL ROLE

As services are delivered in closer proximity to a client's social environment, in the sense of both distance and meaning, the traditional concept of the helping professional as service provider proves increasingly inadequate. We have emphasized the concepts of collaboration and partnership between agency staff and informal helpers throughout earlier chapters; moving from "provider" to "partner" requires a number of basic modifications in the role of the professional. In this chapter we describe the unique features of working with informal helpers that staff in the agencies must take into account as they develop new practice roles. Our discussion emphasizes general principles rather than specific procedures in understanding what a professional may be called upon to do.

Clearly, the amount of change in the professional role required will depend on the strategy chosen, as outlined in Chapter 3. Working with volunteers or the personal networks of clients is more closely related to the traditional direct service role than, for example, working with a neighborhood helping strategy.

The prior training and experience the staff bring to the program will also determine what changes are required. Within the context of our study, the professional staff came from such varied backgrounds that their ideas of the "professional role" did not fall within narrow boundaries. They varied widely in the training, background, and other credentials they brought to their work. Some were high school graduates without formal training, others had college degrees in such diverse areas as sociology, primary education, nursing, recreation, health education, social work, clinical psychology, anthropology, and other fields. Agencies had no standard qualifications for these positions. Some agencies generally required an MSW or related social service degree. Others such as mental health agencies were staffed by several professional disciplines. Still others ran their programs on the model of community action agencies or alternative services where professional degrees were deemphasized.

Developing a Collaborative Role

The process of working with the informal system has a number of unique features which necessitate a rethinking of the role of agency staff. Perhaps the most distinctive features are:

- the lack of clear guidelines for how professionals should interact with informal helpers, and the uncertainty of working with a changing system;
- the need to support informal helpers in their work with "clients";
- the desire to develop community ownership of programs in order that efforts may continue independently without professional help after a limited starting period;
- maintaining a sensitivity to informal helping by understanding its susceptibility to influence and the nature of the incentives which sustain it.

While not all of the programs in our study shared all of these characteristics, there were common experiences that had implications for the professional role.

DEALING WITH UNCERTAINTY

Finding ways to combine professional help with informal help is clearly an exploratory area of practice with new strategies being refined and modified as new situations arise. Very simply, it is a task for which no one can rely on specific training or experience. Thus, supervisors and line staff workers are all obliged to learn "on-the-job."

One of the most common responses is to modify and adapt more familiar practice models to the demands of the new set of goals and objectives. For example, casework in an agency setting with an individual client can be expanded into a personal network strategy, drawing not only on formally structured services but also on the informal resources within the client's social network. For clients lacking an active social network, the worker may see a need for social interaction and support and develop a mutual aid group for a number of such clients utilizing group work skills in the process. A staff member that provides community consultation and education services, on the other hand, may consult with individuals or groups around a specific set of issues in the community, discover a broader need, and, in seeking to expand the scope of the consultation to that larger need, move into a community empowerment strategy.

Given the relative lack of theory and techniques for relating formal programs to informal helping networks, it seems inevitable that human service workers will rely heavily on their previous work and training to sustain their efforts. However, such preexisting methods and techniques may be incompatible with the changing ideology and objectives required in developing partnerships with informal helping networks. In particular, staff ideologies and attitudes toward professional credentials may exercise a major influence on the development of the practice role. The degree to which training and clinical experience are believed to confer a superior status or authority in making decisions about client problems influences staff relationships with informal helpers. To the extent that informal helpers have different ideologies about care, the exclusive reliance of agency staff on professional frames of reference will undermine a collegial relationship.

The lack of clear role guidelines for working with informal helpers tended to influence how staff members for such programs were chosen. Emphasis was often placed on personal characteristics such as flexibility, ability to take initiative, maturity of judgment, and past experience working with the community, rather than on specific credentials. In the absence of more objective qualifications for their position, a number of agency staff, some with professional training and others without, forged a professional identity which reflected to a large extent their personality and life experiences. They were able to relate to other workers, clients, the community, and particularly to informal helpers as individuals, and to evolve strategies for helping people derived from personal understanding and trust. For example, a young black female social worker found her entry into the lives of other black women through common life experiences, as well as through shared racial and sexual identity. Staff who were young mothers of infants related to other young mothers as peers; a young working-class Catholic Italian male gained access to an ethnic working-class Catholic neighborhood due in part to his own knowledge, understanding, and respect for their lifestyle and values. Outside of the confines of the agency, staff are often in a position where "acting natural" will be the most appropriate response to problems (see, Hugman, 1977).

In many cases, working with the informal system requires knowing the community and working in the community rather than the office. This is a process full of uncertainty which involves gaining the trust and acceptance of people in the community and identifying key informal helpers. Both the staff who actually work in the community and the administrators of the agency will be concerned about the effects of their intervention on informal helpers, and the possible repercussions for both the community and the agency. The process of developing a program that works actively with a community is generally a slow one, often agonizingly slow for staff members hoping to see tangible evidence of their efforts. A number of agencies discovered that three to five years were needed to develop effective programs with informal helping networks. The essential elements of the process are developing trust and acceptance in the community, working in a neutral way that does not alienate some segments of the community, and remaining flexible so that the program can respond to the emerging goals perceived by the community. However, there are no standard procedures for accomplishing these tasks.

The ambiguities and tensions that can arise in working with the informal system, particularly when that work involves a relatively unstructured role in the community, led staff in several agencies to develop a staff support group to air frustrations, provide consultation on problems, and define strategies. Peer review among staff can also serve to develop standards that give staff members a way of measuring their own performance and of feeling good about what they are doing, as well as providing guidelines for program development and monitoring. Further, the availability of a support system to staff who are working with informal helping networks can encourage them to continue their efforts. Without peers who provide support or feedback, staff can easily fall back into traditional direct service professional roles. In contrast, staff who spend a great deal of time in the community and who have little contact with other agency staff often become unfamiliar with or even alienated from agency activities. In either case, an important aspect of sustaining work with informal helping systems is for staff to remain integrated and supported by the agency.

Staff have also found it important to move slowly. As one staff person put it, "You have to adopt a style that waits two counts, maybe three counts longer than your natural inclination." There is a temptation to be pulled into mistakes by the need to prove credibility, either to the community or to the agency. The temptation is particularly strong for new, inexperienced staff or when working with communities or groups that have been disappointed by programs before.

Where mistakes are made, as they inevitably will be in an uncertain situation, staff members have found it important to be open in admitting them, whether to others in the agency, the informal helpers, or other community members. Sometimes mistakes can be turned to advantage, but there is almost always some pain and confusion in the process and these feelings must be acknowledged and dealt with.

Staff relationships with helpers also need to remain flexible and able to adjust to changes in the personal circumstances of informal helpers or the helping network. Such changes can come about because helpers experience transitions that lessen their ability or willingness to provide help. People move, change jobs, or simply change in their interests. Such changes can be disruptive to informal helping relationships. Staff responsibilities also change, either within an agency or as the result of turnover. These sorts of changes occur to varying degrees in all programs and are inevitable. Because they can create difficulties in sustaining links with informal helping networks, programs need to identify ways to reduce their impact. Often this is done by continuously identifying and involving new helpers and by giving new staff careful orientation and phasing them in slowly.

SUPPORTING INFORMAL HELPERS

In many of the agencies we studied, staff were working through informal helping networks to achieve benefits for clients and others who were being aided by informal helpers. In some cases staff were involved in providing direct services to clients as well. The process of working through informal helpers gives rise to a conflict between staff feeling responsible for the adequacy and appropriateness of the help given to the client, and feeling that the informal system should continue to work autonomously according to its own standards.

Professional response to the question of how to assure that things are done "correctly" is often based not just on training but also on a number of cultural assumptions and expectations. Indeed, these cultural influences may lead one to assume that training and work experience enhance understanding and knowledge of how to help someone and that certain "techniques" are more effective or more appropriate than others in providing help. Much professional practice relies primarily on close supervision of subordinates by senior professionals to assure adequate performance by junior members of the profession. As such, there is a tendency for agency staff to adopt a similar relationship with informal helpers. In addition, informal helpers may be trained to use the same approach to helping as the professional expert, and are subsequently held accountable for performing certain tasks. Similarly, agency workers may prefer to structure their own role into a bureaucratic time frame and then may oblige those they work with to operate in the same way. For example, a staff member may outline a time for getting acquainted, a time for working together, or a time for ending joint involvement in a much more artificial and limited manner than found in most informal relationships. Thus, the worker uses professional or agency status to formalize and arbitrarily limit and define helping roles.

Some structuring of roles is necessary in order to coordinate the efforts of different people to achieve a common end. However, staff must ensure that the definition of helping tasks and goals is sensitive to the norms of the informal helping networks with which they seek to develop a partnership. Staff in the agencies in our study consistently tried to set mutually determined expectations about the problem to be worked on and the resources to be employed in addressing that problem. For example, an agency that was encouraging the informal helpers of their elderly clients to provide needed care would not contact these helpers without the permission of the client. The client was able to exert some control over the agency's impact on the network, and was encouraged to make the contacts with the informal helpers personally and to have meetings between staff and informal helpers occur in the client's home. Another agency that was working to support those who were primary caregivers for the elderly developed a policy of allowing the caregiver and the client to decide what formal services would be provided. This often meant that the caregiver, usually an adult child or spouse caring for an elderly person, received fewer services than the professional thought were appropriate. In these cases, the importance of allowing the informal helper to decide how much help to ask for was deemed more crucial than professional judgment. Throughout this process, there is a realization that the perceptions of professionals, clients, and informal helpers may be at odds, but each has a valid contribution to make in solving problems.

To be sure, informal helpers often may not define problems in the same way as professionals. They see individuals in the context of a natural setting or set of personal relationships rather than as clients or target populations. They are concerned with meeting their own needs as well as those of the person being helped. This can create a dilemma for staff, since seeing an individual's problems one way may imply taking sides with one set of individuals as opposed to others in the network. For example, in working with frail elderly, staff may find that some relatives see the need for institutionalization while friends who are providing daily assistance disagree. While staff may be working to prevent institutionalization of the client, taking too strong a position on the subject may alienate certain parts of the elderly person's network and may close off access to potential sources of help.

In supporting informal helpers, a staff member is often required to weigh the advantages and disadvantages of being an expert and stepping in versus being a colleague and standing back. Members of a client's personal network may consider themselves responsible but may exercise this responsibility differently than a professional, either more forcefully and with apparent violation of privacy or less directly and with apparent unconcern for the welfare of a particular individual. For example, friends of a chronically mentally ill client may view the client's hallucinations as a normal course of events that will pass if the client is left alone. While this may be the case at times, a professional may interpret the symptoms as self-threatening and feel a responsibility to hospitalize the client. Sometimes the professional standards of staff who enter the informal system are in conflict with general group norms and thus may cause considerable strain or tension if a collaborative relationship is sought. A community subculture where alcoholism is a way of life provides an illustration of a situation that can pose this sort of difficulty.

When professionals and informal helpers are sharing the responsibility for helping, agency administrators and staff must consider the implications of this partnership for their ethical or legal responsibility and liability for care. Can the professional be held responsible if the client does not receive adequate or appropriate care by professional standards? Is the agency responsible if a neighbor helps an elderly client with her laundry and slips down the basement stairs? While this issue is constantly raised by agencies *considering* this kind of program, it was rarely an important problem among those *already working* with informal helpers. A variety of methods had been developed to handle questions of liability. One approach, in line with the philosophy of noninterference with the informal system, was a very nondirective one. While an agency might be involved in linking people who could help or letting it be known that a problem existed and hoping someone would step in, they did not specifically assign tasks to an informal helper, and did not pay the helper. Others were able to find ways to include informal helpers in agency insurance coverage, particularly if an informal helper was providing transportation for a client. Other agencies were simply willing to take the risk, and hope that the issue never arose. In many agencies the question of adequacy of care as judged by professional standards did not arise because the care helpers gave was not considered to require any special expertise. Helpers were encouraged to give the kind of care they were already giving in their everyday lives, rather than medical or therapeutic care for which professional standards were considered to apply.

Confidentiality can also be a problem because of the ethical and, in some cases, legal responsibilities of the professional and the need to protect the privacy of informal helpers and clients. Agency staff have developed several ways of handling the problem. Staff must deal with confidentiality as a general issue early in the relationship with informal caregivers. One way staff deal with the issue is to ask the caregiver never to mention specific names. Another way is for the staff to make an agreement to check with the caregiver before sharing any information with anyone else in the community or with another professional. After the relationship has been established for some time, a general understanding may develop so that each instance need not be discussed. When the agency is offering a service, staff are careful only to reach out to people who have indicated that they want the service. This requires a direct contact so if an intermediary (relative, professional from another agency) makes the referral, staff lets them know they will contact the potential recipient of service directly.

There is another practical issue that is a constant problem among agencies which have chosen to work indirectly through informal helpers rather than or in addition to working directly with the client. The accountability and reporting systems through which staff document their activities generally do not "give credit" for time spent with informal helpers, much less for time spent learning about a community or identifying helpers. Some programs were able to avoid the issue by having enough time spent in direct services to "cover" the time spent in indirect services. Others simply classified the informal helpers as "volunteers," and were then able to fit them into a category considered acceptable by those to whom they were accountable. In the long run, however, a change in policy at a higher level is needed that defines work with informal helping as a legitimate part of a professional role.

BUILDING COMMUNITY OWNERSHIP

A common goal among the thirty agencies was to build a program that could eventually function independently with little or no professional support. This goal implied that the program be designed so that control could be transferred from professionals to the community, and so that informal helpers could be helped to develop the necessary competence to take control. In other cases the informal systems grew and developed during the course of collaborative efforts in ways not originally foreseen by the staff. Initially, staff acted as a catalyst or organizer among clients and helpers. While the network was developing a sense of purpose or identity, members expected staff to provide direct assistance. As the network developed further and members began to take ownership of activities, staff moved to a less active role, in which they provided consultation or backup support. Staff had to be alert to changes that signalled a need for a new strategy. For example, one program involved in developing a mutual aid network for the frail elderly found that elderly in boarding homes were being increasingly excluded as the group became more formalized. Staff undertook additional efforts to provide a separate support system for the institutionalized elderly.

Even for agencies intending to create an autonomous program, the path is not easy. It was not unusual for programs to have a relatively high level of funding at the beginning, perhaps through demonstration funding, and to lose sight of their long-term goal of self-sufficiency when designing the program. Thus, a program might be designed that was simply too scattered geographically, too ambitious, or too heavily dependent on expensive support services such as transportation to be picked up by the informal helpers. Agency staff who were successful at "spinning off" independent programs tended to keep this goal constantly in mind in making day-to-day decisions.

MAINTAINING A SENSITIVITY TO INFORMAL HELPING

There are a number of other aspects of the role of informal helping networks in services which have implications for the professional's role. Understanding what informal helpers may be expected to do, how informal helping may change when it comes into contact with formal services, and what incentives may sustain or undermine informal helping networks represent considerations that agency staff must incorporate into the roles they have defined for themselves.

By selectively supporting certain behaviors and values, professionals unquestionably influence the nature of informal helping. Informal helpers seem to have a built-in advantage of credibility, but they do not always have the skills or knowledge to help as effectively as they might. Professionals, therefore, need not be apologetic for their interventions as long as they are aimed at increasing effectiveness and are not destructive of this credibility—intentionally or otherwise. The informal helpers' consciousness of their helping role and the implications of their helping activity generally increase with professional contact.

The provision of financial resources for informal helpers can raise issues of accountability to the agency and put pressures on the informal helpers to behave less naturally or change the way they think about the help they provide. It can also cause competitiveness among the helpers. For these reasons, most agency staff conclude that monetary payments should be avoided where possible. Informal helpers may have their own ways of handling payments, however, which help to protect their sense of what they are doing. One group of helpers said that the monthly stipends they were paid to reach out to new widows kept them from having to seek other employment, but that the work they were doing with widows was based entirely on their own interest and concern. Another group said the money was to pay them to keep records—something they hated to do and would not do otherwise—rather than to help others. Another program paid informal helpers from among a network of chronically mentally ill persons but rotated the position in the network every six to nine months to prevent the professionalization of the helper. Payments can be problematic but they can be justified when the tasks of helping are potentially burdensome.

A major dilemma in providing payment is that money or other material resources may be most important to the support of informal helping activities among the most impoverished. Who provides the diapers in an informal day care arrangement may not be important in affluent circumstances, but may make or break the relationship among low-income mothers. It is precisely where such resources are most needed and valued that they can be most disruptive and divisive. Since there are instances where the absence of resources is a deterrent to helping, more thought needs to be given to how such resources can be provided constructively.

Agency staff have also learned that it is vitally important for them to be circumspect in gauging the types of demands they make on informal systems of support. Where and how an agency taps into the informal system has far-reaching implications, not only for the kind of partnership that can be developed, but also for the future direction the informal helping will take. People's sense of obligation for one another and confidence in their ability to be helpful is influenced by professional interventions. One faction in a community may be given added resources and legitimacy through their contact with staff which may affect the local balance of power. Indeed, someone who is not really helpful may gain status and credibility by being associated with the program.

Informal helpers may encounter different role expectations in their contact with agency staff than they are used to in their daily lives. An essential part of the professional's relationship with the helper is to understand the helper's readiness or ability to accept certain tasks or take responsibility for helping others. For example, parents who have successfully adjusted to having a developmentally disabled child may not be ready to support other parents during their adjustment. Likewise, a person who has been active in developing social or recreational opportunities for the elderly may not be ready to advocate for low-income housing for the elderly. Staff must be sensitive to a helper's willingness and ability to take on new or expanded helping roles; otherwise there is a risk that the helpers may become disenchanted or frustrated with what they feel others expect of them or what they come to expect of themselves.

The role of agency staff is also influenced by changes that occur within an informal helping network. Some helpers increasingly idr "fy with the agency in which staff are working, as the way in which staff involve them in their work instills in them some professionalized conceptions of helping. Sometimes helpers come to be seen by staff as informal leaders and are asked to serve on task forces and advisory boards. Similarly, some mutual aid networks continue indefinitely on an informal and spontaneous basis, while others become increasingly formalized and adopt an independent status as a legally constituted organization with elected leadership. Changes such as these are neither necessarily positive or negative, although the character of the helping may lose or gain certain attributes. The question for staff is whether this change is appropriate in the context of program objectives, whether it is beneficial (or at least not harmful) to the helping process, and whether new or additional efforts need to be undertaken.

Conclusion

The need to modify traditional professional roles in working with informal helpers arises out of the differences between the two systems of helping. The intent of the discussion has been to identify some of the potential conflicts that can occur in the roles defined for informal helpers and describe where staff may need to reconsider their professional roles in relating to informal sources of support. As we gain respect for the differences between informal and formal support and recognize the possible conflicts that blending them may engender, we can combine the efforts of professionals and informal support networks to mutual benefit in a more planned and focused way. The agencies we have studied highlight the sources of difficulties and provide some lessons about how they can be accommodated by professional staff in practice. These lessons by no means provide a comprehensive blueprint for action, but they do suggest a number of strategies that have been successfully implemented.

The experiences of the agencies we have studied provide a perspective which contrasts sharply with more traditional attitudes that have defined informal caregivers as handmaidens of professionals or as unruly nuisances. The most difficult choice this new perspective presents to the professional is that of deciding whether or not to renegotiate the balance between public and private responsibilities for care. We must be prepared to question whether the assumption of public or professional responsibility also implies an equivalent assumption of control over the process of caregiving. The perspective provided by our study of agency experience is that responsibility and control can be shared to a greater extent than has been done in the past, through a partnership between formal and informal sources of help. This partnership is best served when the parties to social and health care stand on an equal footing.

Chapter 9

THE PROSPECTS FOR PARTNERSHIP

Advocates of systems of community-based services often predicate their policies on a belief in the value of a comprehensive continuum of formal and informal sources of care. We have been suggesting throughout this book that a more appropriate metaphor may be the idea of two worlds of care, each with its own norms, standards, and means of self-perpetuation. To be sure, bridges can be built between the two worlds; partnerships can be established between professionals and informal helpers. But such partnerships can only be successful when there is a genuine sharing of responsibility and control. In the preceeding chapters we have tried to spell out what this sharing implies at the level of program and practice. In this final chapter we take a broader view, discussing various concepts of community care and presenting some guidelines that may be useful to those who want to reshape formal services into a collaborative effort with informal caregivers. We also highlight some of the major issues that will be of concern to professionals seeking a partnership.

Care with the Community

Although the idea of community care has become popular, it has come to mean many things to many people. For example, one view articulates a model in which explicitly structured, publicly supported professional services are provided locally in communities and neighborhoods. The focus is on developing professional services *in* the community with debate centering on the appropriate location, arrangement, and dispensing of formal caring resources. Considerable attention is given to the administrative arrangements necessary to orchestrate the system such as: mechanisms for ensuring efficiency and accountability in operations; case management and client tracking systems to guarantee continuity in care; and ways to establish local, state, and federal intergovernmental cooperation. The responsibility for providing care remains in the public domain, where client needs are met in a continuum of way stations from hospital to home and professionals wait ready to administer their remedies at each point. To the extent that the community becomes involved in this model of community care, it traditionally has been by formal invitation or induction either as advisors on boards, volunteers under supervision, or recipients of support or advocacy services.

A contrasting orientation to community care is held by advocates of the model of care *by* the community. This position sees more localized services as a further incursion of government into private life. Community care as they see it should emphasize strengthening the caregiving capacity of the community directly through "the cultivation of effective informal caring activities within neighborhoods *by* local residents themselves—discovering, unleashing, supporting and relying upon indigenous caring agents and locally-rooted helping networks" (Abrams, 1980:12). Community involvement and control would eclipse the public and professional role for direct caregiving although there is still ground left open for professional responsibility. This responsibility would consist of legitimizing and developing linkages among neighborhood associations and community organizations, and fostering religious support systems, support found in the workplace, in medical care settings, in criminal justice settings, and in schools as well as helping to create other specialized self-help groups and mutual aid networks.

These two orientations imply quite different conceptions of what needs and resources are. The first sees the need for an expanded public role in the wake of a perceived breakdown in traditional family functions and social institutions, while the second views such expansion as undermining and misappropriating the community's capacity for care (Moroney, 1976). They also reflect different responses to questions of responsibility for care and how this responsibility is best carried out. Care *in* the community promises equity and reliability by making public agencies responsible for meeting need, while care *by* the community attempts to insure responsiveness and self-determination; in many ways each sacrifices things for which the other argues.

Since neither position is tenable in the extreme, the idea of care *with* the community looks for a policy choice "in between the aimless wandering of communal life and the authoritarian direction of the community . . . not a compromise between the two extremes, but an entirely new approach" (Sennett, 1970:103). The agencies we have studied offer illustrations of how such an approach might develop. A balance between more localized formal services and stronger informal systems might be struck by fostering arrangements of shared responsibility for care among professionals, families, and community members (Moroney, 1976; Parker, 1980).

The implication of the programs we have studied is that shared responsibility is possible and that it can result in services of high quality, broad coverage, and finely tuned sensitivity to the needs of the recipients. In order to achieve a partnership, however, changes are required in the way professionals conceive of their role and in the way services are organized.

FUNDAMENTAL PRINCIPLES

A number of common principles thread through our discussion of the experiences of agency staff in developing a partnership with informal helping networks. While these principles find different expression depending upon whether the task is providing support for an individual client or advocating for rights in a community, in their most general form they provide the wellspring for policies promoting a partnership. Among the more critical points of emphasis are:

- Seeing clients as individuals with strengths and resources as well as problems and needs. Formal and informal resources should be brought to bear only when the individual's resources fall short of meeting the needs and only as a supplement, not as a replacement.

- Recognizing the importance to individuals of an enduring network of social relationships. Interventions should incorporate a sensitivity and respect for different conceptions of helping and the specific understanding of particular relationships in order to strengthen the network.

- Recognizing that, while professional and informal caregivers may make different contributions to social care, equality of status should prevail. In practice, shared decision-making, mutual respect, and collegiality are often indicators of equality between professional staff of an agency and informal helpers.

- Sharing responsibility for care. An attempt is made to balance roles and responsibilities such that professional care is neither intrusive nor neglectful while opportunities and incentives for informal helpers encourage their involvement without resulting in burden.

- Respecting the way individuals and local groups define their problems and attempting to find solutions that match the reality as defined by those who must deal with the situation rather than solutions that reflect an artificially limited definition of target problems or needs.

At the basis of these principles is a willingness on the part of professionals and agencies to open themselves up to a true partnership with the community. This requires a willingness to negotiate means and ends and a flexibility of response that may be at odds with the rationalistic, centralized mode of program planning, administration, and evaluation that is currently popular. It also means that the philosophical orientation with which the task is approached is more important than the techniques and procedures presumed by a specific program model.

MODIFYING PRACTICE

The successful implementation of these principles will also be influenced by certain attributes of the agency's organization and management and the way that professional staff are utilized. Our study suggests that for the staff to develop partnerships with informal helping networks they must have sufficient flexibility to respond to situations as they occur, as well as having a degree of autonomy to make decisions appropriate to the different constraints and opportunities involved in balancing client needs with informal resources and agency services. Because of the emphasis on finding local solutions to individual needs and the necessity of staff autonomy, the management style of the system of agency services must accord a greater amount of front line decision-making authority. Decentralization of authority is, in large measure, a result of the need to delegate responsibility to those who have the most complete information about the kinds of contributions informal helping networks might make. Further, linking formal agency resources with informal caring networks can best be accomplished in the context of a local area owing to the complexities involved in understanding what might be available in the local community as well as establishing a credible identity with community members.

As we have suggested, many of these elements which facilitate work with informal helpers will involve a change in traditional modes of program practice. Many existing human service agencies may need to reorient their approach to service provision. The following changes may be required:

- Changing the traditional service provider role to emphasize the direct provision of services less and increase the support given to family and community caregiving roles;
- Allowing greater use of agency facilities and resources by informal helpers;
- Revamping accountability and reporting requirements to accurately reflect the work done by and with informal helpers;
- Increasing outreach to community groups and informal helpers. This may involve establishing a team approach or increasing the use of paraprofessional staff;
- Expanding the use of referral agreements with other agencies;
- Basing services and caseloads on geographical areas;
- Developing coordination mechanisms which provide for a "neutral turf" in negotiating the integration of public, voluntary, and informal resources.

From a broader view, these changes suggest that the promotion of a partnership will be best accomplished within existing human service systems by emphasizing policies of gradual decentralization, destandardization and deprofessionalization (Gladstone, 1979). Rather than a strategy of dismantling formal services, this position argues that formal services are still vital but better provided within organizational conditions that are more likely to respond to the demands of working closely with local communities. It must also be recognized that finding the organizational and managerial arrangements which provide suitable conditions for a partnership of care with the community creates other problems. A review of earlier experiences in promoting locally based services (O'Donnell &

Sullivan, 1974), service integration (Gans & Horton, 1975), flexibility and autonomy in staff roles (Leighninger, 1980), and decentralization policies (Aldrich, 1978) suggests that these strategies are not without their hazards to coordination and accountability, among other things.

OTHER OPTIONS

That organization, management, and professional reorientation will not provide all the answers demands that we jointly pursue other policy strategies. One possibility is to look for various incentives that might promote more shared responsibility; for example, providing agency staff with a budget constraint for each client and allowing them to provide financial incentives to informal helpers (Challis & Davies, 1980), changing zoning or code regulations that inhibit self-help or providing tax incentives to promote family care (Gollub & Waldhorn, 1979). It will be difficult, however, to find incentives that can be effective without commercializing informal relationships or disrupting them. As another alternative, some are attracted to the idea that the promotion of greater shared responsibility may come from the creation of expanded opportunities for local governance, arguing that "good clients make bad citizens" and what we really need are good citizens (Dewar, 1978). Local solutions to local problems might come from fostering the development of groups and associations within the community that are sufficiently empowered to participate or otherwise make an impact on formal service delivery (Berger & Neuhaus, 1977).

Assessing the Capacity of Informal Helping

If we are to fully consider the prospects for a partnership, we must assess the capabilities of the informal sector as well as those of formal agencies. Here, the objective is not to discover what changes might need to be made, since, by definition, informal caregiving is not organized in such a way that directed changes are possible. Rather, the objective is to assess the inherent limitations of informal caregiving in order to judge its capacity for equal partnership. Is there a risk that the promotion of self-help and informal sources of support will provide a justification for reduced expenditures for social welfare? Could the informal sector "take up the slack" by providing more care than it already does? On whom would the burden actually fall? The prospect of a partnership also raises questions of quality and adequacy: How does the quality of care provided informally compare to that provided by professionals? Whose needs are met and whose are not?

These questions ask us to apply the same policy criteria used in evaluating formal systems of services to the care provided informally. Standards of efficiency, effectiveness, equity, and adequacy give us ways of measuring the appropriateness of professional human services. Are these standards which should also be expected to be maintained under conditions of shared responsibility with informal helping networks? Can a partnership in care address these policy criteria without requiring that informal care be essentially a system that parallels formal services? These are questions which merit serious investigation. We can discuss several areas to illustrate the issues involved in maintaining standards of care in a partnership.

MAINTAINING INDIVIDUAL RIGHTS

The corollary of increasing acceptance of public responsibility for social and health needs is the greater accordance to citizens of rights to social services. In many areas, ideologies have shifted from believing that individual needs derived from moral weakness or personal failing to believing that many problems are beyond personal control and seeing individuals as victimized by birth, fortune, or society. As reparation for being victimized, according to this argument, individuals have a right to services from the state as *parens patriae* (Kittrie, 1971). Without questioning the wisdom of citizens' rights to human services, the idea of a partnership with a shared responsibility for care can raise concerns about whether these rights can be maintained. Will efforts to promote a partnership be seen as a way to avoid providing services? Do those who are cared for informally have the same rights as those who are served by professionals?

Several studies that have looked into the process of how people utilize both formal and informal helping resources highlight some of the issues that policy makers will need to consider in dealing with questions of individual rights to care. A series of studies of help-seeking behavior among a large sample of Chicagoans explored the limits of informal helping (Lieberman & Glidewell, 1978). Most people in this survey were found to use *both* formal and informal helping resources. In one study, respondents more often sought help from informal helpers than from formal sources for a wide range of problems. Health related problems were the exception where formal sources of help (usually physicians) were preferred (Brown, 1978). No differences in sex or marital status were found to distinguish rates of informal help seeking, but racial differences (black women were more likely to contact informal associates than white women) and age distinctions (respondents over 60 years old showed a decrease in reliance on informal help) were present. Respondents under greater stress were more likely to turn to formal as well as informal sources out of a reluctance to continue to rely solely on informal associates for assistance. It seems, then, that there are circumstances under which people prefer to seek help from formal agencies even though informal help is very important.

Second, informal help may not be more accessible, in an emotional sense, than formal help. Another study in this series looked into the norms related to informal help and found that only about half of the respondents who received help from informal sources felt they had a right to expect such help (Schreiber & Glidewell, 1978). Even fewer working-class respondents felt they had such rights. Further, rights differed according to the nature of the problem and the type of help; few respondents felt they had a right to economic assistance, for instance. The norm of reciprocity seemed to provide a backdrop to people's sense of rights and obligations: "Even in the most personally emotionally supportive relationships within a family, there was a vague residual concern: was one indebted or not? It was uncomfortable to place oneself in debt, even for emotional support, even within the family. It was often unclear just what one's rights were" (Schreiber & Glidewell, 1978:452). The tenuous claim that many persons seemed to feel they had on informal sources of help urges caution in estimating the extent to which such assistance may be counted on.

Two further studies on the Chicago sample shed some light on the perceptions of recipients concerning the relative effectiveness of informal help. One study focused on how parents sought help for concerns surrounding their young adult children (Menaghan, 1978) and found no relationship between reported relief obtained from help and the type of helper chosen, i.e., formal or informal. The nature of help (e.g., whether listening, insight, or action) seemed the determinant of relief rather than who provided it. Relief was also more often obtained when a combination of both formal and informal help was received. The second study looked at a wider range of problems and a broader sample in examining the adaptive consequences of help (Lieberman & Mullen, 1978). After controlling for demographic variables, access to help, event perception and personal resources, the study failed to find a consistent relationship between respondent outcome and type of help obtained. These studies suggest that informal help is evaluated by recipients as no worse (or better) than formal help. A combination of the two seems most effective.

Although these studies do not provide the final word on how people feel about informal helping, they point up the kinds of issues that policy makers will need to consider in promoting shared care. In particular, if we are to pursue a policy of shared care between formal and informal sources of help, we need to consider the possibility that people may not want to seek informal help for some problems and the norms of informal helping may undermine people's willingness to call upon informal helpers or influence their perception of the reliability of informal support. The quality and appropriateness of the informal help provided to people with varying degrees of need should be evaluated as carefully as help from formal sources. Clearly the rights of those receiving help in a community care system should be the same regardless of whether professional or informal sources of care are brought into play. If we expect professionals to satisfy clients' needs, we should also be prepared to ask whether informal supports are equally satisfying. We may run the risk of infringing on privacy in dealing with these issues, but we should not base our policies on the naive assumption that informal care does not carry costs of its own.

MAINTAINING THE ADEQUACY AND QUALITY OF CARE

In Chapter 2, we showed the variety of types of assistance informal helping networks can provide to individuals with different needs. Among the agencies we studied, informal helpers who were being supported by staff often represented the major source of care for potential clients, many with severe problems. While our study has shown that informal caregivers play a major role in effectively meeting a broad spectrum of needs, we clearly need to give careful consideration to how policies of shared responsibility may need to be modified for different problems and populations. In particular, we need to be concerned about how adequately different needs are covered. Can informal sources of care be directed to all types of problems or are they more suitable for some needs and less for others? We must also consider the quality of informal care for different types of problems. Do all participate in the benefits of informal care equally? Very simply, we need to know more about the question: Who cares for whom? This question takes on further significance when we think about the special needs of populations who are often thought of as most appropriate for community care: the old, the young, and the dependent. At the very least, these individuals' problems are much more severe than the range of stresses and strains faced by a general population. Since needs for support are great among these populations, we need to appreciate who is now providing informal care and how they are responding to the demands placed on them. Informal caregiving has costs for the giver as well as the recipient.

Aside from the observations in our study, further evidence on the identity of informal caregivers can easily lead one to the conclusion that the phrase, "networks of informal helping" is really a euphemism for wives, mothers, and daughters (Abrams, 1980). To be sure, as we discussed in Chapter 2, informal helpers are not always women nor are they always immediate family members. However, the vast bulk of care received by the chronically impaired is provided principally by family members (National Center for Health Statistics, 1972) and women are the primary "kin-keepers" (Lieberman, 1978:496). Two recent British studies focusing on the informal caregivers of dependent individuals give insight into the experience of providing support.

One study identified 120 caregivers within a general population that cut across both urban and rural areas (Equal Opportunities Commission, 1980). More than 60 percent of those identified were caring for an elderly relative, another 25 percent were caring for a disabled adult, with the remainder caring for a handicapped child. Female caregivers (usually mothers, wives, or daughters) outnumbered male caregivers (usually husbands) three to one. Most caregivers were providing extensive help with activities of daily living (e.g., shopping, cleaning, transportation) as well as companionship and emotional support. The effect of providing care on the caregivers' lives was telling. More than one-quarter experienced profound economic limitation—having to give up a job altogether, cutting back in hours worked, or having to forego job advancement. Most experienced a financial burden in meeting the extra costs associated with transportation needs, special foods, clothing, and various aids. Needless to say, the social life of the informal caregiver was severely curtailed and family stress was greatly pronounced.

Another study looking at informal caregivers of 100 long-term psychiatric patients generally confirms these findings (Lonsdale, Flower & Saunders, 1980). Here, women outnumbered men two to one as caregivers and almost two-thirds were married to the patient; parents, siblings, children, and friends comprised the remaining one-third. Fewer than one-third did not live with the patient and most of these lived in the same building or neighborhood. The majority of caregivers (two-thirds) reported being the primary source of support, receiving no help from other relatives; only a minority felt that formal services could be relied on if they were not able to provide care. The impact of providing care was significant: one-third reported financial hardship, one-half reported diminished health and well-being from being tired, anxious, depressed, or nervous. These effects were more pronounced for those caregivers of patients with more severe problems.

A common finding of both studies was that caregivers helped out of a sense of moral responsibility, that their understanding of the problems they were attempting to care for diverged from that of professionals, and that they were often unaware or mistrustful of available services. The experience of the informal caregivers revealed by these studies indicates the extent of the burden placed on informal caregivers with the potential consequences for family isolation, breakdown and ultimate rejection of a dependent member (see Kreissman & Joy, 1974). The studies also point up the potential pitfalls of basing care on the assumption of moral responsibility not only because of the likelihood that this may become a burden to the caregiver (with implications for the resulting experiences of the cared for) but also because this responsibility seems to be disproportionately taken on by women. This is not to suggest that we raise a suspicious eyebrow about those who act on moral obligation but rather to ask whether this is by choice, particularly since the obligation seems to severely limit one's social and economic opportunities. If we are serious about developing a partnership with informal caregivers in a community care system, we need to begin to consider the disadvantages that seem to attend the experience of providing informal support for the dependent and to find a more equitable distribution of the tasks of being supportive. We can help to reduce exploitation, rather than tacitly encouraging it, by developing a better understanding of the demands made on informal caregivers (Parker, 1980); for instance, for how long will it be necessary to provide care, what will be the appropriate intensity and complexity of caring tasks, will the situation get better or worse? We also need to understand the conditions which foster a fairer allocation: "Once we bring ourselves to see care as an essentially calculative involvement, we can go on to ask a large number of questions about the specific sorts of calculation that will make specific sorts of caring worthwhile to specific sorts of people" (Abrams, 1978:86).

In the final analysis, we must also come to terms with the limits of informal caregivers and with the realization that in some situations, formal resources must be brought to bear. Our study suggests possibilities for interweaving professional resources so that informal caregivers may be adequately supported. That support for caregivers must be given with sensitivity is underlined by the experience of providing formal home-based care for the elderly. Often, professional resources served as a formal substitution for informal care with the result that it was not particularly effective, did not relieve stress on informal caregivers and was not equally sensitive to different populations at risk (Dunlop, 1980). On balance, the overriding issue here is how standards of effective care can be assured among informal caregivers. Recognizing that informal caregiving activities may only be attractive under conditions of limited liability (Leat, 1979), will an attempt to promote community care strengthen the effectiveness of informal caregivers on their own terms or reconstruct informal support to fit a conception of effective care quite incompatible with the terms of informal caring relationships?

DESIGNING APPROPRIATE ROLES FOR INFORMAL HELPING

The process of ensuring that the social rights of those in need are protected and that standards of care are maintained without unduly burdening the informal helpers hinges most critically on the role assumed by informal helping networks in participating in a partnership with professionals and human service agencies. What much of the process of developing appropriate roles for informal helping networks comes down to is a decision about what purpose is to be served by promoting partnerships. The partnership may fail even if the strengths and weaknesses of the informal helpers are clearly understood and the agency has prepared itself adequately simply because it is expected to serve conflicting purposes.

In the past, informal helpers or their equivalents have been considered to serve such purposes as being "bridges" to the poor (Levine et al., 1978) or providing cost-effective substitutes for professionals (Davies, 1980). While the list of roles for nonproviders in the design and execution of public human service programs has been growing, there has also been growing confusion about what purpose this involvement is to serve (Rosener, 1978). Citizen participation initiatives which mandate task forces, citizen boards, or consumer input have proliferated alongside the incorporation of volunteers, lay providers, or indigenous leaders in the provision of agency services. The more institutional view continues to see the public as clients. Thus, within a single agency, one may imagine a public role that is at once a governor, provider, and recipient.

Within the context of the partnership we have described earlier, an informal helper may play all these roles at the same time. Policy makers must be aware of the tension between conflicting purposes and their potential consequences of role ambiguity and strain for informal helpers. For example, one effort may involve informal helpers in order to facilitate the identification of unrecognized needs and services. Another effort may work with informal caregivers to support and reinforce existing patterns of helping so as to reduce the need and consequent demand for professional intervention. In both instances, the types of helpers identified may be similar but the roles defined for them by agency staff are quite inconsistent. In practice, these alternative purposes will be incompatible since "action taken to promote [one] will create conditions and circumstances inimical to the development of the other" (Tucker, 1980:26).

Thus, each program purpose will define a role for informal sources of support that implicitly emphasizes only *some* of the skills and attributes of informal helpers, offers only *some* of a broad range of possible opportunities for participation, and provides incentives that encourage only *some* of a wide range of informal helping activities. Very simply, whom we choose to involve, what we ask them to do, and what we are prepared to contribute are the major questions that underlie what we can expect to gain from informal sources of support.

Toward a Partnership

The intent of this review of the potential obstacles to a true partnership between professionals and informal helpers has not been to show that such a partnership is impossible. On the contrary, it is our belief that care *with* the community is the most viable and productive direction for the future development of human services. We have presented these cautions in order to provide guidance for the development of viable policies for community care.

Policy makers will need to be concerned with the demands made on informal caregivers and the community as well as on professionals and the formal sector, and in some ways will need to advocate for both sides. If too much emphasis is given to the virtues of informal care with the result that people are left to "get on with it," informal caregivers will be overburdened and community needs unmet; likewise, emphasis on professional responsibility and control as a way to assure reliability and equity may undermine the contributions made willingly by informal caregivers and may prove insensitive to individual needs and situations.

Equity, efficiency, accountability, responsiveness, and involvement are benefits few would not want reflected by any policy of community care. The trouble is, these criteria must be translated into strategies for action at which point we are likely to find that not all may be achieved at once. The competing expectations about care and the dilemmas they raise are not just matters confronted by policies of shared responsibility and escaped by pursuing alternative policy orientations, however. Tradeoffs among competing values are implicit in any policy proposal. Very simply, something cannot be everything. In this respect, the prospects for creating a partnership depend on a better recognition of where and how the process of compromise may be approached. Experimentation with a view toward tolerating a pluralistic diversity in matching needs and resources and mutual respect for the different contributions professionals, clients, and informal caregivers can make to community care may provide a useful foundation to begin this process. Since complexity and conflict are also likely to be abiding characteristics of the process, we might usefully adopt a perspective that accepts the legitimacy of untidiness. On this point, Schiller's comments in 1797 on the excesses of the French Revolution may provide a timely guide: "The political or educational artist must learn to approach his medium with genuine respect for its individuality and potential for dignity . . . and beware of damaging its natural variety" (in Gladstone, 1979:123).

While informal helping networks must be approached with respect for their natural variety, they are not particularly fragile. Agencies should not hesitate to propose partnerships for fear of causing damage to existing informal networks. People have been helping each other for a long time and they are likely to continue to do so with or without recognition from the formal sector. The style and form of informal helping will continue to change according to shifting social forces such as changes in the relative proportion of different age groups, patterns of migration, family roles, economic conditions, and the like. Agencies will need to be sensitive to these changes and adapt their practices accordingly, but both forms of helping are here to stay and have much to gain from close cooperation.

It is the obligation of publicly supported human services and the helping professions to be responsive to those clients, citizens, and communities who provide them sanction. Establishing a partnership of responsibility for care between helping networks and human service agencies is fundamental to promoting this responsiveness. A new partnership in responsibility will be well served by policies that *recognize* the important role to be played by informal sources of help, *reaffirm* this role in the arrangements and procedures of systems of organized professional services, and *respect* the diversity of values and exchanges that are the strength of informal helping networks.

APPENDIX A: METHODOLOGY

Our study was undertaken to identify, analyze, and describe the experiences of human service agencies which were in the process of learning how informal systems work and how they might be supported or strengthened. For this purpose, we began with a conceptual framework to guide our research questions. The conceptual framework outlined the major components of each system of care, formal and informal.

As shown in Figure A, the study focused on programs within agencies that were working in some way with the informal system. Such programs could be a small part of the agency's function or include the entire agency. The relationships that other agencies in the formal system had with both the local agency and the informal network were studied to a lesser extent. The major elements of the informal system considered were (a) the members of the system, who might be helpers, recipients of help, or both; (b) the nature of the exchange among members; and (c) the neighborhood context of the network, when applicable.

The primary focus of our research was on the interaction between the two systems; we were particularly concerned to learn more about what forms such interaction might take. Our research questions for this aspect of the study examined how each part of the two systems might relate to others.

- What were the agency's goals and objectives in working with informal helping networks?

- What program strategies were being utilized by agencies to bring professional and informal sources of care together?

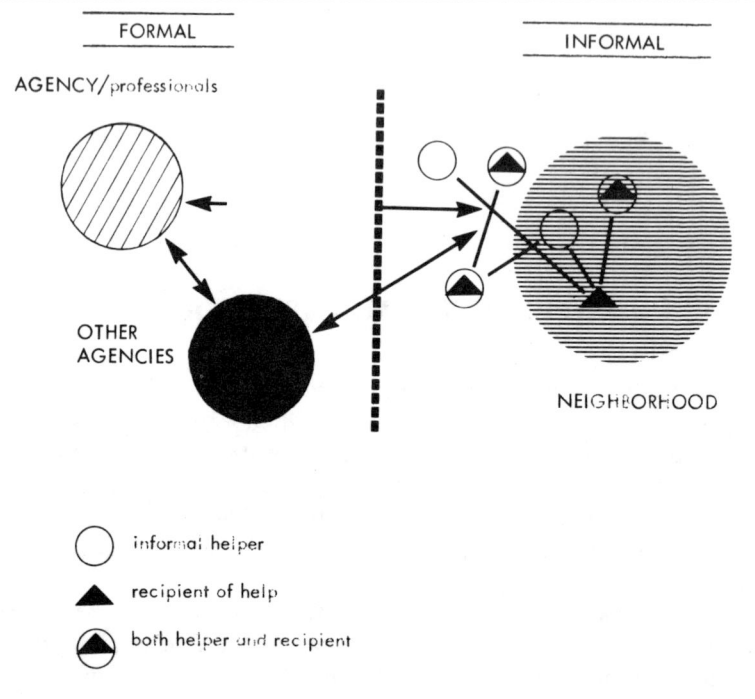

Figure A   Community Service System

- What were the respective roles and responsibilities of professional staff and informal caregivers in these efforts?
- How was interaction influenced by characteristics of the agency or the professional staff?

We also looked at how interaction might be influenced more directly by broader aspects of each system. For example,

- Were helping networks influenced by the neighborhoods and communities in which they were found?
- Do such variations change the way agencies or professionals could interact with informal sources of care?
- How did the overall service system in a community influence the ability of an agency to work with the informal system?

- Could the informal system make an impact on services in the community?

Research Methods

We conceived of our study as an exploratory effort to identify and describe the scope of activities that agencies were involved in and the approaches which had been developed to work with different problems and populations and in different settings. As a result, we wanted to identify programs that were *illustrative* rather than *representative* of how professionals might work with informal helping networks, feeling that this strategy would be less likely to ignore particularly innovative developments in the field. Further, given the lack of any systematic framework for describing all possible programs, there was no satisfactory basis for judging how a particular program might be representative.

SAMPLE DESIGN AND SELECTION

A pool of possible programs was identified through reviews of the literature, personal contacts and referrals, advertisements in professional or program media with national circulation, and recommendations of individuals working in the field. Identified programs were sent a brief questionnaire asking for a program description and any available brochures or written materials. The sample of thirty agencies was selected from the 66 programs identified as plausible candidates for study.

In developing the sample, it was necessary to address the question of what was unique about informal helping networks. We addressed this issue of uniqueness by focusing more particularly on the kind of helping that occurs within helping networks, and on an examination of helping networks as a set of exchanges with common norms and expectations. Thus, for the purposes of studying programs that were working with informal helping networks, selection criteria were developed that focused on the nature of help provided rather than on structural features of the network or agency characteristics.

The selection of programs to be included in the study involved a two-stage screening process. The first stage involved the selection of ten programs for in-depth study and description. A normative model for screening the programs was generated by the research team after review of the literature in this area. In looking at program descriptions, assessments were made on each of the following dimensions:

Agency
- Operates with paid staff whose principal occupation is to provide services to agency clients;
- Provides direct services or conducts activities related to human service objectives;
- Program operational (past initiation-idea stage), with funding continuing at least through the life of the research study.

Staff-Helper Interaction/Relationships
- Staff view informal helpers with whom they work as colleagues or peers, and respect their role in "delivering" services.
- Staff seek to reach a broader client group, albeit indirectly, by working with helpers.
- Staff are sensitive to and respect cultural norms of the helpers or helping network with which they are working.

Network
- The informal system involves exchanges based on supporting or helping the individual client, rather than exchanges solely of material goods or political actions.
- The informal system relies on voluntary and reciprocal exchanges of help, in contrast to paid or "therapeutic" exchanges.
- Exchanges occur in the indigenous setting of the network rather than in agency facilities.

Since we were interested in determining how broadly the idea of professional collaboration with informal helping networks could be extended, we also selected programs to achieve a diversity among the types of problems or target populations that were being served as well as differences among agency settings and community contexts. This consideration led us to relax some of our ideal expectations regarding informal helping networks and their relationship with agency staff. It became clear that for some problems or client populations and in some community contexts, helping networks might be absent or unable to provide sufficient care. In such instances, agency staff may have had to emphasize more structure in attempting to foster new sources of informal support than we had anticipated in our ideal model. Thus, programs were selected that came as close as possible to meeting ideal expectations while also reflecting a wide dispersion of problem focus and setting.

The first ten programs selected for study were employed as a test of the normative model. From the experience of observing the first stage sample, we were able to refine our ideas of the range of variation to be included in the sample. Based on our experience with the first ten programs, two additional factors were incorporated into sample selection: the general approach to working with informal helping networks and the problem focus of the program. Four general approaches were identified and can be described briefly:

Neighborhood networks—the agency works with a locality-based network of natural helpers, residents, or opinion leaders; this category was subsequently split into two different approaches— neighborhood helping and community empowerment;

Personal networks—the agency works with members of an individual client's network such as family, friends, and neighbors;

Mutual support networks—the agency works with a group of individuals whose helping relationship is based on shared circumstances or characteristics and mutual concerns;

Volunteer linking—the agency matches individual helpers with clients to provide informal help. (While this approach may overlap with the more traditional volunteer approach, the emphasis is on mutual helping, noninstitutionalized roles, and personalized relationships.)

The range of problem foci chosen for inclusion in the sample were comprehensive in order to contrast how approaches may differ in implementation according to different target population needs and problem settings. Agencies were selected that were working with the following target populations: the elderly; children, youth and families; developmentally disabled and handicapped; psychiatrically disabled; and the general community. These populations differ in the generality or specificity of their problems and also in the types of help and support needed.

Table 1A presents the distribution of the thirty programs according to the problem focus of the agency, the size of the agency staff and the location (urban/rural). The agencies are geographically dispersed across fifteen states in the continental United States and range from urban inner city Manhattan to small towns in several states. In addition, they also vary in size, some operating within large, complex

TABLE 1A   Sample Distribution

| | Agency Size and Setting | | | | |
| | small | | large | | |
Problem Focus	urban	rural	urban	rural	TOTAL
Elderly	1	1	6	1	9
Children, Youth and Families	3	1	1	0	5
Developmentally/physically disabled	3	0	1	0	4
Mental health related	1	0	3	2	6
Community related	1	2	3	0	6
TOTAL	9	4	14	3	30

Note: Small—less than 15 paid staff
Large—16+ paid staff

organizations and others having only one or two paid staff members. The distribution among these three major factors of problem focus, size, and setting is fairly even, permitting exploratory analysis of the effects of these factors on the task of combining formal and informal helping resources.

DATA COLLECTION

The principal method of data collection for this study was an in-depth guided interview conducted by research staff with agency staff during the course of a one- to three-day visit to the agency. The interview(s) followed a discussion guide and covered six major topics including:

- characteristics of neighborhood/community
- agency characteristics
- program descriptions
- staff-helper interactions
- helper characteristics
- evaluations of program strengths and weaknesses

The discussion guide was ten pages long and took a minimum of four hours to cover completely. Program staff were given a copy of the discussion guide prior to the arrival of the interviewer. The guide was divided into questions to be answered by administrators (or program managers/supervisors), by program staff (line-level), and by the informal helpers.

Interviewers were expected to guide the interview/discussion, probe responses, and serve as the vehicle through which the program descriptions were related back to the general open-ended questions contained in the discussion guide. In order to accomplish this task, the research team worked closely together to develop common understandings of the research questions. All interviews were recorded via detailed notes, often accompanied by a tape-recording. These were either transcribed or translated back into answers to the questions contained in the discussion guide and supplemented by available written descriptive materials (brochures, program reports, contact logs, and so on) provided by the program staff.

DATA ANALYSIS

Because agency data took many forms from statistical reports to interview notes to qualitative descriptions by research staff, several modes of data analysis were pursued. First, each agency was described by means of a case study. Case study descriptions were returned to each agency for internal staff review and correction. Modifications were made where appropriate to ensure the validity and accuracy of the case study report.

Variable construction proceeded from content analysis of project materials and from review of case study descriptions. Data items were categorized into variables and rating scales developed for several areas of analysis, including characteristics of the overall agency, the program strategy, the informal helpers, and the neighborhood or community. Each set of data items was rated by research staff for agencies they had responsibility for site visiting. While some of the data called for specific categorical responses or quantitative raw scores, most items required a rating on a four-point scale to assess relative frequency or presence of a characteristic. Scored data sets were coded in machine readable form and computerized for ease of analysis.

The ratings were developed for levels of aggregation (as some agencies had developed several program strategies and some were working with several different neighborhoods), while for others neighborhood factors were irrelevant. Thus, three levels of aggregation were differentiated—agency, program, and neighborhood. That is, some variables were rated separately for each agency, some for each program strategy within an agency, and some for each neighborhood in which the program operated.

Each agency was rated by only one of the research staff—that person who had first-hand knowledge of the agency and who was felt to possess the most complete knowledge of agency data. Since no other individual was in a position to confirm the research staff member's rating, an alternative test for rater bias was employed. Agencies were classified into groups corresponding to the staff member responsible for scoring agency information. The resulting groups were compared along major analytic variables to determine whether or not systematic relationships between rater and data item scores were present. No significant relationships were found by this method.

Analysis of data sets was usually conducted independently with respect to each level of aggregation. In addition, cross-level analyses were performed to compare agency level factors with approach level factors. To assess the presence of spurious cross-level weightings (e.g., one agency having a large number of approaches), analyses were done two ways: (1) by repeating agency characteristics for each approach in a pooled approach analysis; and alternatively (2) by averaging approach characteristics for each agency in agency pooled analysis. The results of each procedure were compared to confirm or deny the stability of relationships.

Given the exploratory nature of the sample and the variety of ways in which each program differed from the others in the sample, tests of significance were treated with caution. More often, the statistical procedures of choice were those which permitted pattern inspection: factor analysis, clustering, and discriminant function analysis. However, for many essentially descriptive purposes, univariate and bivariate statistical analyses were performed. We also found it essential to augment and in some instances shape the use of statistical analysis with case descriptions from agency notes. Often specific illustrations of program practice, anecdotes about informal helpers, and opinions of staff formed the strongest base of information for judging the conceptual validity of the analysis. Thus, the methods of study were primarily qualitative and exploratory, although quantitative evidence was used where possible to supplement our findings.

APPENDIX B: CASE STUDY DESCRIPTION

Case No.	Target Population	Location
1	Elderly	small, midwestern town
2	Elderly	medium sized western city
3	Elderly	rural counties in northeast
4	Elderly	large, eastern city
5	Elderly	large, eastern city
6	Elderly	eastern, suburban area
7	Elderly	large, western city
8	Elderly	large, western city
9	Elderly	large, southwestern city
10	Families	medium-sized western city
11	Families	large, western city
12	Families	medium-sized midwestern city
13	Families	large, western city
14	Families	eastern suburban area
15	Physically handicapped	large, southwestern city
16	Developmentally disabled	medium-sized western city
17	Developmentally disabled	large, western city
18	Developmentally disabled	large, western city
19	Developmentally disabled	large, eastern city
20	Preventive mental health	small southwestern town
21	Chronically mentally ill	large, southeastern city
22	Preventive mental health	rural eastern counties
23	Mental health	urban and rural midwestern county
24	Chronically mentally ill	four urban and rural, midwestern counties
25	Preventive mental health	large midwestern city
26	Neighborhood housing and health	medium-sized southern city
27	Community mental health	small western town
28	Community mental health	large, midwestern city
29	Community health and mental health	midwestern, rural Indian reservation
30	General community improvement	large, western city

		Strategies				
Case No.	Agency	Personal Network	Volunteer Linking	Mutual Aid	Neighborhood Helping	Community Empowerment
1	small demonstration project	X		X	X	
2	small senior center				X	
3	community mental health center				X	
4	large, private agency	X		X		
5	large, private sectarian agency	X	X		X	
6	community mental health center			X		
7	private settlement house	X		X	X	
8	branch of large senior center	X		X		
9	middle-sized ethnic agency				X	
10	small demonstration project			X		
11	small demonstration project			X		
12	branch of statewide private program		X	X		
13	small, private agency			X		
14	large, private child guidance agency		X	X		
15	large, private agency		X	X		
16	middle-sized private agency		X	X		
17	small, private agency		X			
18	one site of a 3-site, statewide demonstration project		X			
19	private, mental health agency			X	X	
20	branch of community mental health center	X			X	
21	large, state agency			X		
22	demonstration project at state university				X	
23	community mental health center			X	X	
24	small private agency		X	X		
25	branch of large private settlement house			X	X	
26	city government				X	
27	small demonstration program	X			X	X
28	small demonstration program			X		X
29	demonstration project at college				X	X
30	large, private service agency	X		X	X	X

REFERENCES

Abrams, P. Community care: Some research problems and priorities. In J. Barnes & N. Connelly (Eds.), *Social care research*. London: Bedford Square Press, 1978.

Abrams, P. Social change, social networks and neighborhood care. *Social Work Services*, 1980, *22*, 12-23.

Adams, J. Inequity in social exchange. In L. Berkowitz (Ed.), *Advances in experimental social psychology*. New York: Academic Press, 1965.

Aldrich, H. Centralization versus decentralization in the design of human service delivery systems. In R. Sarri & Y. Hasenfeld (Eds.), *The management of human services*. New York: Columbia University Press, 1978.

Andrews, E., & Norton, D. *Neighborhood self-help project*. Chicago: Chicago Commons Association, 1979.

Armstrong, K. *How can we avoid burnout?* Paper presented to Second Annual Conference on Child Abuse and Neglect, Houston, April 1977.

Barker, R., & Associates. *Habitats, environments and human behavior*. San Francisco: Jossey-Bass, 1978.

Bayley, M. *Mental handicaps and community care*. London: Routledge & Kegan Paul, 1973.

Bayley, M. Community orientated systems of care. *Occasional Papers Series*. Berkhamsted, England: Volunteer Centre, 1978.

Bell, W. Relatives' responsibility: A problem in social policy. *Social Work,* 1967, *12*, 32-39.

Berger, P., & Neuhaus, R. *To empower people: The role of mediating institutions*. Washington, DC: American Enterprise Institute for Public Policy Research, 1977.

Berkeley Planning Associates. *Evaluation of child abuse and neglect demonstration project 1976-1977. Final report*. Springfield, VA: NTIS, NCHSR 78-65, 1977.

Berkowitz, L. Social norms, feelings and other factors affecting helping and altruism. In L. Berkowitz (Ed.), *Advances in experimental social psychology*. New York: Academic Press, 1972.

Biegel, D., & Naperstek, A. *Neighborhood and family services project—first year report*. Washington, DC: Washington Public Affairs Center, 1979.

Biegel, D., & Spence, B. *Human service policy recommendations to the National Commission on Neighborhoods*. Washington, DC: Washington Public Affairs Center, 1978.

Brown, B. Social and psychological correlates of help-seeking behavior among urban adults. *American Journal of Community Psychology,* 1978, *6,* 425-440.

Cantor, M. Life space and the social support system of the inner city elderly of New York. *Gerontologist,* 1975, *15,* 23-26.

Challis, D., & Davies, B. Community care of the elderly: A new approach. *British Journal of Social Work,* 1980, *10,* 1-18.

Cochran, M., & Brassard, J. Child development and personal social networks. *Child Development,* 1979, *50,* 601-616.

Coit, S. *Neighborhood guilds.* London: Swan Sonnenschein, 1892.

Cole, J., & Frieden, L. *Transitional living: A program fostering community integration of severely handicapped persons.* Houston: Texas Institute for Rehabilitation and Research, June 1977.

Collins, A., & Pancoast, D. *Natural helping networks.* Washington, DC: National Association of Social Workers, 1976.

Collins, A., & Watson, E. *The day care neighbor service.* Portland, OR: Tri-County Community Council, 1969.

Cox, F., & Garvin, C. The relation of social forces to the emergence of community organization practice: 1865-1968. In F. Cox, J. Erlich, J. Rothman & J. Tropman (Eds.), *Strategies of community organization.* Itasca, IL: Peacock Publishers, 1972.

Craven, P., & Wellman, B. The network city. *Sociological Inquiry,* 1973, *43,* 57-88.

Curry, R., & Young, R. D. *Socially indigenous help: The community cares for itself.* Paper presented at the meeting of the American Psychological Association, Toronto, September 1978.

Cutler, D. Volunteer support networks for chronic patients. In L. Stein (Ed.), *Community support systems for the long term patient.* San Francisco: Jossey-Bass, 1979.

Davies, B. *The cost-effectiveness imperative, the social services and volunteers.* Berkhamsted, England: The Volunteer Centre, 1980.

Dearlove, J. The control of change and regulation of community action. In National Institute on Social Work (Ed.), *Community work.* London: Routledge and Kegan Paul, 1974.

Dewar, T. The professionalization of the client. *Social Policy,* Jan. 1978, 4-9.

Downs, A. *Inside bureaucracy.* Boston: Little, Brown, 1967.

Dunlop, B. Expanded home-based care for the impaired elderly: Solution or pipe-dream? *American Journal of Public Health,* 1980, *70,* 514-519.

Durkheim, E. *The division of labor in society.* New York: Macmillan, 1933.

Durman, E. The role of self-help in service provision. *Journal of Applied Behavioral Science,* 1976, *12,* 433-444.

Eddy, W., Paap, S., & Glad, D. Solving problems in living: The citizen's viewpoint. *Mental Hygiene,* 1970, *54,* 64-72.

Edmonson, E., Bedell, J., & Gordon, R. The community network development project: Bridging the gap between professional aftercare and self help. In F. Reissman & A. Gartner (Eds.), *Mental health and the self help revolution.* New York: Human Services Press, 1980.

Ehrlich, P. *Mutual help for community elderly demonstration and research project, Volume 1, Final report.* Carbondale, IL: Rehabilitation Institute, Southern Illinois University, 1979.

Emlen, A. Realistic planning for the day care consumer. In National Conference on Social Welfare (Ed.), *Social Work Practice.* New York: Columbia University Press, 1970.

Equal Opportunities Commission. *The experience of caring for elderly and handicapped dependents.* Manchester, England: Author, 1980.

Erickson, J. The concept of personal networks in clinical practice. *Family Process,* 1976, *14,* 487-498.

Etzioni, A. *A comparative analysis of complex organizations* (Rev. ed.). New York: Free Press, 1975.

Field Research Corporation. *In pursuit of wellness.* Report to the Office of Prevention, Department of Mental Health, State of California, 1979.

Fischer, C. *Networks and places.* New York: Free Press, 1977.

Froland, C. Formal and informal care: Discontinuities in a continuum. *Social Service Review,* 1980, *54,* 572-587.

Froland, C., Pancoast, D., Chapman, N., & Kimboko, P. *Professional partnerships with informal helpers: Emerging forms.* Paper presented to the American Psychological Association, New York, September 1979.

Gallup, G. Strong neighborhoods offer hope for the nation's citizens. *The Gallup Poll,* March 1978.

Gans, H. *The urban villagers.* New York: Free Press, 1962.

Gans, S., & Horton, G. *Integration of human services.* New York: Praeger Publishers, 1975.

Gershon, M., & Biller, H. *The other helpers.* Lexington, MA: Lexington Books, 1977.

Gladstone, F. J. *Voluntary action in a changing world.* London: Bedford Square Press, 1979.

Gollub, J., & Waldhorn, S. *Local governance approaches to social welfare problems.* Menlo Park, CA: SRI International, 1979.

Gottlieb, B. The development and application of a classification scheme of informal helping behaviors. *Canadian Journal of Behavioral Science,* 1978, *10,* 105-115.

Gouldner, A. The norm of reciprocity: A preliminary statement. *American Sociological Review,* 1960, *25,* 161-178.

Gourash, N. Help seeking: A review of the literature. *American Journal of Community Psychology,* 1978, *6,* 413-425.

Greenberg, M. A theory of indebtedness. In K. Gergen, M. Greenberg & H. Willis (Eds.), *Social exchange: Advances in theory and research.* New York: John Wiley, 1976.

Hall, R. *Organizations: Structure and process* (2nd ed.). Englewood Cliffs, NJ: Prentice-Hall, 1979.

Harlow, E. Sexual liberation doesn't always mean freedom. *Working Woman,* June 1979, pp. 47-52.

Hirsch, B. Natural support systems and coping with major life changes. *American Journal of Community Psychology,* 1980, *8,* 153-166.

Homans, G. *Social behavior: Its elementary forms.* New York: Harcourt Brace Jovanovich, 1961.

Hugman, B. *Act natural.* London: Bedford Square Press, 1977.

Janowitz, M., & Suttles, G. The social ecology of citizenship. In R. Sarri & Y. Hasenfeld (Eds.), *The management of human services.* New York: Columbia University Press, 1978.

Joyner, P. *Followup data on community facilitators.* Unpublished manuscript. Durham, NC: Durham Community Development Agency, 1978.

Kanfer, F. Personal control, social control and altruism. *American Psychologist,* 1979, *34,* 231-239.

Katz, A., & Bender, E. *The strength in us.* New York: Franklin Watts, 1976.

Keller, S. *The urban neighborhood.* New York: Random House, 1968.

Kittrie, N. *The right to be different: deviance and enforced therapy.* Baltimore: Johns Hopkins Press, 1971.

Kreissman, D., & Joy, V. Family response to the mental illness of a relative: A review of the literature. *Schizophrenia Bulletin,* 1974, *10,* 34-59.

Kulka, R., Veroff, J., & Douvan, E. Social class and the use of professional help for personal problems: 1957 and 1976. *Journal of Health and Social Behavior,* 1979, *20,* 2-17.

Leat, D. *Limited liability?* Berhamsted, England: The Volunteer Centre, 1979.

Leighninger, L. The generalist-specialist debate in social work. *Social Service Review,* 1980, *54,* 1-12.

Lenrow, P. Dilemmas of professional helping. In L. Wispe (Ed.), *Sympathy, altruism and helping.* Cambridge: Harvard University Press, 1976.

Levine, M., Tulkin, S., Intagliata, J., Perry, J., & Whitson, E. *The paraprofessional: A brief social history.* Unpublished manuscript. Department of Psychology, SUNY—Buffalo, March 1978.

Lieberman, G. Children of the elderly as natural helpers. *American Journal of Community Psychology,* 1978, *6,* 489-498.

Lieberman, M., Borman, L., & Associates. *Self-help groups for coping with crisis.* San Francisco: Jossey-Bass, 1979.

Lieberman, M., & Glidewell, J. Overview: Special issue on the helping process. *American Journal of Community Psychology,* 1978, *6,* 405-413.

Lieberman, M., & Mullan, J. Does help help: The adaptive consequences of obtaining help from professionals and social networks. *American Journal of Community Psychology,* 1978, *6,* 499-517.

Litwak, E. Agency and family linkages in providing neighborhood services. In D. Thursz & J. Vigilante (Eds.), *Reaching people: The structure of neighborhood services.* Beverly Hills, CA: Sage Publications, 1978. (a)

Litwak, E. Organizational constructs and mega bureaucracy. In R. Sarri & Y. Hasenfeld (Eds.), *The management of human services.* New York: Columbia University Press, 1978. (b)

Litwak, E., & Szelenyi, A. Primary group structures and their functions: Kin, neighbors and friends. *American Sociological Review,* 1969, *34,* 465-481.

Lonsdale, S., Flowers, J., & Saunders, B. *Long term psychiatric patients: A study in community care.* London: Personal Social Services Council, 1980.

Lubove, R. *The professional altruist.* Cambridge: Harvard University Press, 1965.

Menaghan, E. Seeking help for parental concerns in the middle years. *American Journal of Community Psychology,* 1978, *6,* 477-488.

Michael, D. *On learning to plan and planning to learn.* San Francisco: Jossey-Bass, 1973.

Moroney, R. M. *Family and the state: Considerations for social policy.* London: Longman, 1976.

Moroney, R. M. Families, social services, and social policy: the issue of shared responsibility. *NIMH studies in social change.* Washington, DC: D. H. H. S. #(ADM) 80-846, 1980.

National Center for Health Statistics. *Home care for persons 55 years and over.* Washington, DC: Vital and Health Statistics Series 10 No. 73, DHEW, (HSM) 72-1062, 1972.

National Commission on Neighborhoods. *People, building neighborhoods. Final report to the President and the Congress of the United States.* Washington, DC: U. S. Government Printing Office, 1979.

O'Donnell, E., & Sullivan, E. Service delivery and social action through the neighborhood center: A review of research. In H. Demone & D. Harshberger (Eds.), *Human service organizations.* New York: Behavioral Publications, 1974.

Pancoast, D., Froland, C., & Collins, A. Informal support for the chronic mental patient. *Journal of the National Association of Private Psychiatric Hospitals,* 1980, *11* (5), 42-47.

Parker, A. *Consumer participation in health programs.* Unpublished manuscript. School of Public Health, University of California—Berkeley, January 1972.

Parker, R. A. *The state of care.* Unpublished manuscript. Department of Social Administration, University of Bristol, April 1980.

Perlman, J. Grassrooting the system. *Social Policy,* 1976, *7* (2), 4-21.

President's Commission on Mental Health. *Report of the Task Panel on Community Support Systems.* (Vol. 2, Appendix). Washington, DC: U. S. Government Printing Office, 1978.

Riessman, F. How does self help work? *Social Policy,* 1976, *7,* 41-45.

Rosener, J. Matching method to purpose. In S. Langton (Ed.), *Citizen participation in America.* Lexington, MA: Lexington Books, 1978.

Rosenhan, D. Learning theory and prosocial behavior. *Journal of Social Issues,* 1972, *28,* 151-164.

Rubin, D. *California state policy toward 'non-traditional healing arts'.* Unpublished manuscript. School of Public Policy, University of California—Berkeley, December 1975.

Santiago, L. From settlement house to antipoverty program. *Social Work,* 1972, *17* (4), 73-78.

Sarri, R., & Hasenfeld, Y. (Eds.). *The management of human services.* New York: Columbia University Press, 1978.

Schon, D. *Network-related intervention.* Unpublished manuscript prepared for the Networking Conference, sponsored by the School Capacity for Problem-Solving Group, National Institute of Education, Washington, DC, August 1977.

Schreiber, S., & Glidewell, J. Social norms and helping in a community of limited liability. *American Journal of Community Psychology,* 1978, *6,* 441-453.

Sennett, R. *The uses of disorder: Personal identity and city life.* New York: Vintage Books, 1970.

Smith, C., & Freedman, A. *Voluntary associations.* Cambridge: Harvard University Press, 1972.

Smith, G. *Social work and the sociology of organizations.* London: Routledge & Kegan Paul, 1970.

Smith, S. *Natural systems and the elderly: An unrecognized resource.* Portland, OR: Regional Research Institute for Human Services, Portland State University, 1975.

Snyder, P. Z. Neighborhood gatekeepers in the process of urban adaptation: Cross-ethnic commonalities. *Urban Anthropology,* 1976, *5,* 35-51.

Stack, C. B. *All our kin.* New York: Harper & Row, 1974.

Staub, E. Instigation to goodness: The role of social norms and interpersonal influence. *Journal of Social Issues,* 1972, *28,* 131-150.

Sussman, M. Relationships of adult children with their parents in the United States. In E. Shanas & G. Streib (Eds.), *Social structure and the family.* Englewood Cliffs, NJ: Prentice-Hall, 1965.

Thibaut, J., & Kelley, H. *The social psychology of groups.* New York: John Wiley, 1959.

Thomas, R. *Professional roles in working with social support systems: Competition or cooperation?* Paper presented at the Sixth Annual Summer Program on Mental Health Education, Madison, Wisconsin, July 1979.

Toseland, R., Decker, J., & Bliesner, J. *A community outreach program for socially isolated older persons.* Unpublished manuscript. San Diego: San Diego Youth Services, 1979.

Tracy, G., & Gussow, Z. Self-help health groups: A grass roots response to a need for services. *Journal of Applied Behavioral Science,* 1976, *12,* 381-396.

Trimble, D. A guide to the network therapies. *Connections,* 1980, *3* (2), 9-21.

Tucker, D. Coordination and citizen participation. *Social Service Review,* 1980, *54,* 13-30.

Warren, R., & Warren, D. *The neighborhood organizer's handbook.* Notre Dame, IN: University of Notre Dame Press, 1977.

Webber, M. Order in diversity: Community without propinquity. In L. Wingo (Ed.), *Cities and space: The future use of urban land.* Baltimore: Johns Hopkins Press, 1963.

Wellman, B. The community question: The intimate networks of East Yorkers. *American Journal of Sociology,* 1979, *84,* 1201-1231.

Wingspread Report. *Strengthening families through informal support systems.* Racine, WI: The Johnson Foundation, 1978.

Wirth, L. Urbanism as a way of life. *American Journal of Sociology,* 1938, *44,* 3-24.

Wispe, L. Positive forms of social behavior: An overview. *Journal of Social Issues,* 1972, *28* (3), 1-19.

Wolfenden Report. *The future of voluntary organizations.* London: Croom Helm, 1978.

Young, M., & Willmott, P. *Family and kinship in East London.* London: Routledge & Kegan Paul, 1957.

Zaltman, G., Duncan, R., & Holbek, J. *Innovations and organizations.* New York: John Wiley, 1973.

Zimmer, A. *Strengthening the family as an informal support for their aged.* Paper presented at the meeting of the Gerontological Society, Dallas, November 1978.

ABOUT THE AUTHORS

Charles Froland, D. P. H., is an Assistant Professor at the School of Social Work and Research Associate at the Regional Research Institute for Human Services at Portland State University. He served as the project director of the national study of agencies reported in this book. In related work, he has conducted a comparative study of the informal support systems of four groups of mental health clients and has written several journal articles on the role of social networks in mental health and health care. Dr. Froland has designed and administered research and evaluation studies in a wide number of social welfare program areas including child abuse and neglect, delinquency prevention, vocational rehabilitation, income maintenance, and drug and alcohol services. He has also conducted two studies of community care in the United Kingdom.

Diane L. Pancoast, M.S.W., is a social worker and a Research Associate at the Regional Research Institute for Human Services, Portland State University. She served as principal investigator on the Natural Helping Networks and Service Delivery project. With Alice H. Collins she wrote *Natural Helping Networks* (1976), which has become an important source book in this developing field of social work. In addition to her involvement in the OHDS project, she is currently engaged in research on the social support networks of persons with epilepsy. She has recently applied the networking model to the problem of child abuse and neglect in a chapter of the book *Supporting Families and Protecting Children* (Garbarino & Stocking, 1978). Ms. Pancoast also teaches a class on Natural Helping Networks to graduate social work students and has consulted widely on this topic.

Nancy J. Chapman, Ph.D., is an Associate Professor in the School of Urban Affairs at Portland State University, and served as co-principal investigator of the Natural Helping Networks and Service Delivery project. A social and environmental psychologist, her involvement in the field of social networks includes teaching a graduate seminar in urban social networks and research on the effects of the physical and social characteristics of the neighborhood on the well-being of the elderly. In addition, she has studied the concept of privacy, privacy and neighboring in multiple family housing, and has developed a trade-off approach to assessing the environmental needs of families living in public housing.

Priscilla J. Kimboko, B.A., is currently a Research Associate at the Regional Research Institute for Human Services at Portland State University. With an undergraduate degree and graduate work in anthropology, she is now completing her dissertation for a Ph.D. in Urban Studies at the School of Urban Affairs at Portland State University. Her doctoral program and research focus on the impacts of social change on families, social networks, and organizations. She has worked as a research assistant on a study which looked at the impact of divorce on children and parents, on the Natural Helping Networks and Service Delivery project, and is currently involved in a longitudinal study of the adjustment of new stepparent families.